EXPLORE

GREEK MYTHS!

Anita Yasuda
Illustrated by Mike Crosier

Recent language arts and social studies titles in the **Explore Your World!** Series

Nomad Press
A division of Nomad Communications
10 9 8 7 6 5 4 3 2 1

This book was manufactured by Marquis Book Printing,
Montmagny, Québec, Canada
October 2016, Job #125547

ISBN Softcover: 978-1-61930-450-5
ISBN Hardcover: 978-1-61930-446-8

Educational Consultant, Marla Conn

Questions regarding the ordering of this book should be addressed to
Nomad Press
2456 Christian St.
White River Junction, VT 05001
www.nomadpress.net

Printed in Canada.

CONTENTS

Interested in primary sources? Look for this icon.
Use a smartphone or tablet app to scan the QR code and explore more! You can find a list of URLs on the Resources page.

If the QR code doesn't work, try searching the Internet with the Keyword Prompts to find other helpful sources.

TIMELINE & MAP

These dates are approximate.

2000 BCE: The Minoans build large palace complexes on Crete, including one at Knossos that some believe may have belonged to legendary King Minos.

1600 BCE: The Minoan civilization collapses after the Santorini volcano erupts.

1600 BCE: The Mycenaean culture develops on mainland Greece, known as Hellas.

1250 BCE: According to legend, the Greeks use the Trojan Horse to defeat the city of Troy after a 10-year siege.

776 BCE: The first Olympic Games take place.

750 BCE: The first Greek alphabet develops.

700 BCE: Homer composes the epic poems *The Iliad* and *The Odyssey*.

700 BCE: Hesiod writes *Theogony* and *Works and Days*.

650 BCE: Sparta becomes the most powerful city–state in Greece.

534 BCE: Theater begins to thrive in Greece.

510 BCE: Democracy begins in Athens.

500 BCE: The Classical Period begins in Greece.

500 BCE: Pindar writes poems set to music called *odes*.

490-480 BCE: Greek city–states defeat invaders from the Persian Empire.

460 BCE: The First Peloponnesian War between forces led by Sparta and Athens begins.

432 BCE : The Parthenon, a large temple to Athena on the Acropolis in Athens, is finished.

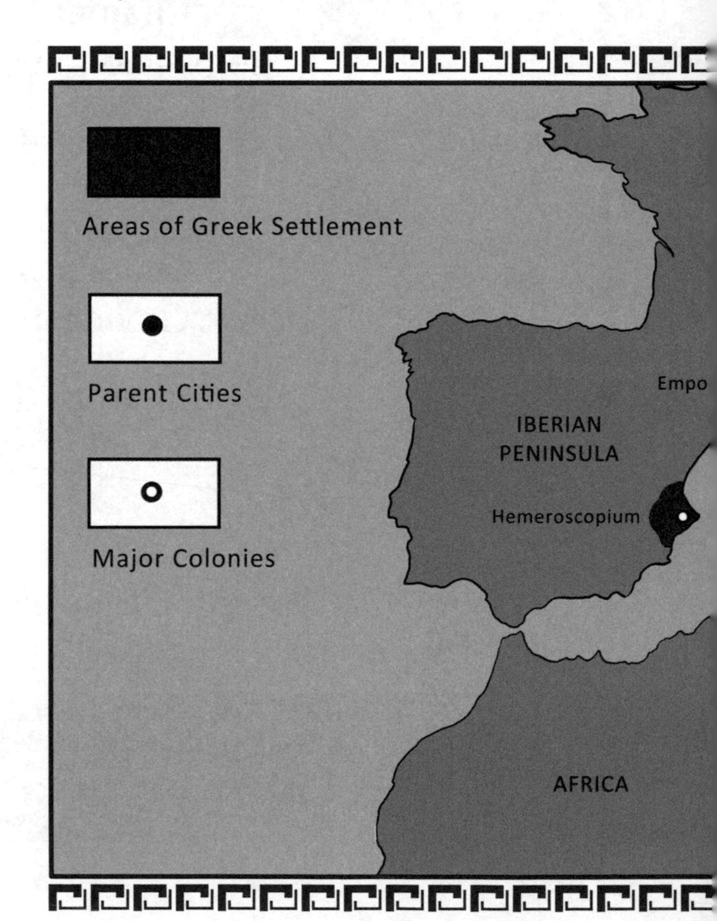

TIMELINE & MAP

431 BCE: The Peloponnesian War breaks out again.

404 BCE: Sparta defeats Athens.

380 BCE: Plato begins teaching philosophy, mathematics, and astronomy in a grove near Athens.

338 BCE: King Philip II of Macedon (now northern Greece) conquers Greece.

336 BCE: Alexander the Great, son of King Philip II, becomes king.

332 BCE: Alexander the Great dies at the age of 32.

260 BCE: Archimedes describes how a lever works.

146 BCE: Rome conquers Greece. For many years, Romans have adopted the Greek gods and goddesses and renamed them.

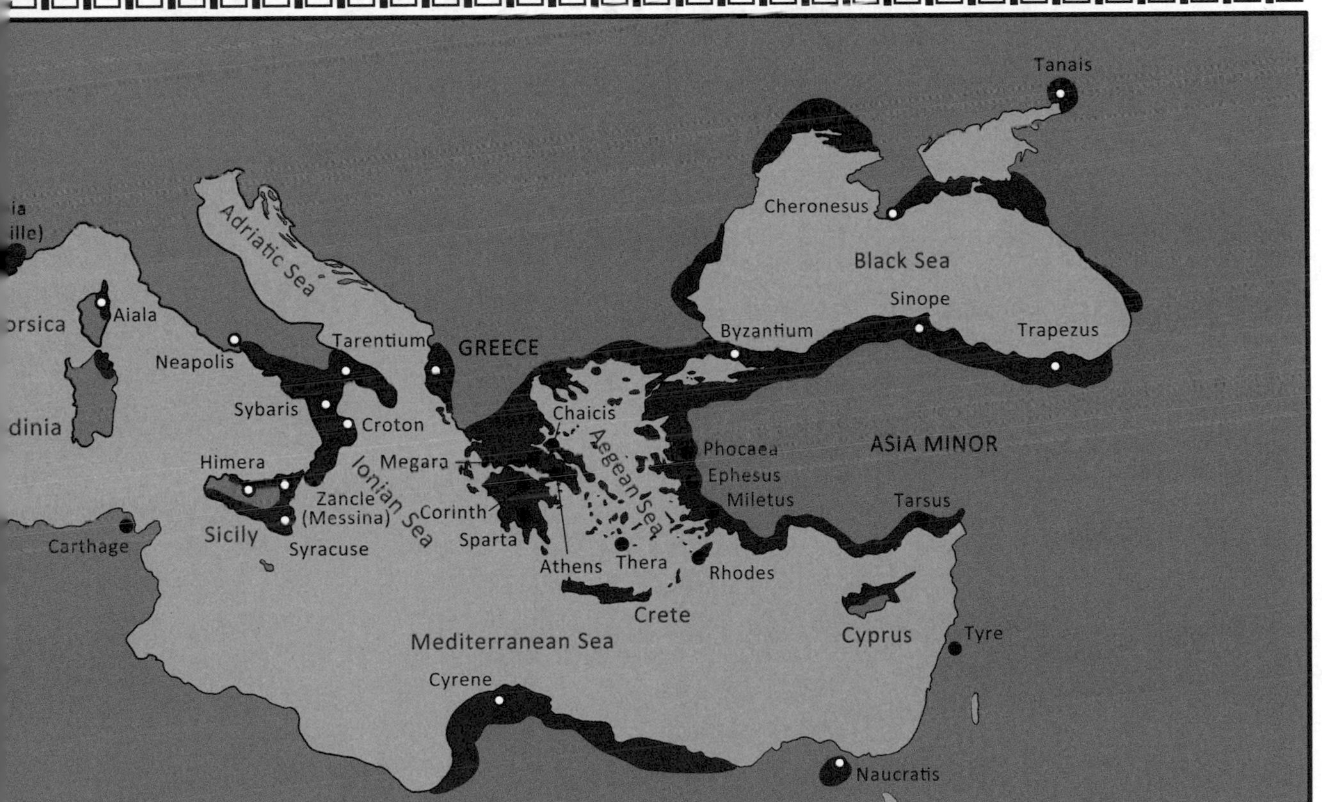

Acropolis
epic
myth
culture
archaeologist
Ionic
Mycenaean Age
toga
frieze
ode
oracle
rituals
furrow
Olympic Games
Mount Olympus
citizen
trident
fresco
civilization
democracy
immortal
altar
Doric
Titan
discus
Corinthian
demi-god
polis
prophecy
jury
ark
gorge
philosopher
literature
Dark Age
axis
stoa
shrine
pediment
Boustrophedon
covenant
compound pulley
narcissism
exiled
astronomy
forge
harmony
zodiac
riddle
Norse
pantheon
quarry
lever
pulley
constellation
chaos
satyr
manga
mortar
lever
patron
pivot
offering
sacrifice
curse
lyre
votive
plain
geography
compass rose
society
Peloponnese
orchestra
Persian Empire
Northern Hemisphere
Southern Hemisphere
ostraka
tectonic plate
supernatural

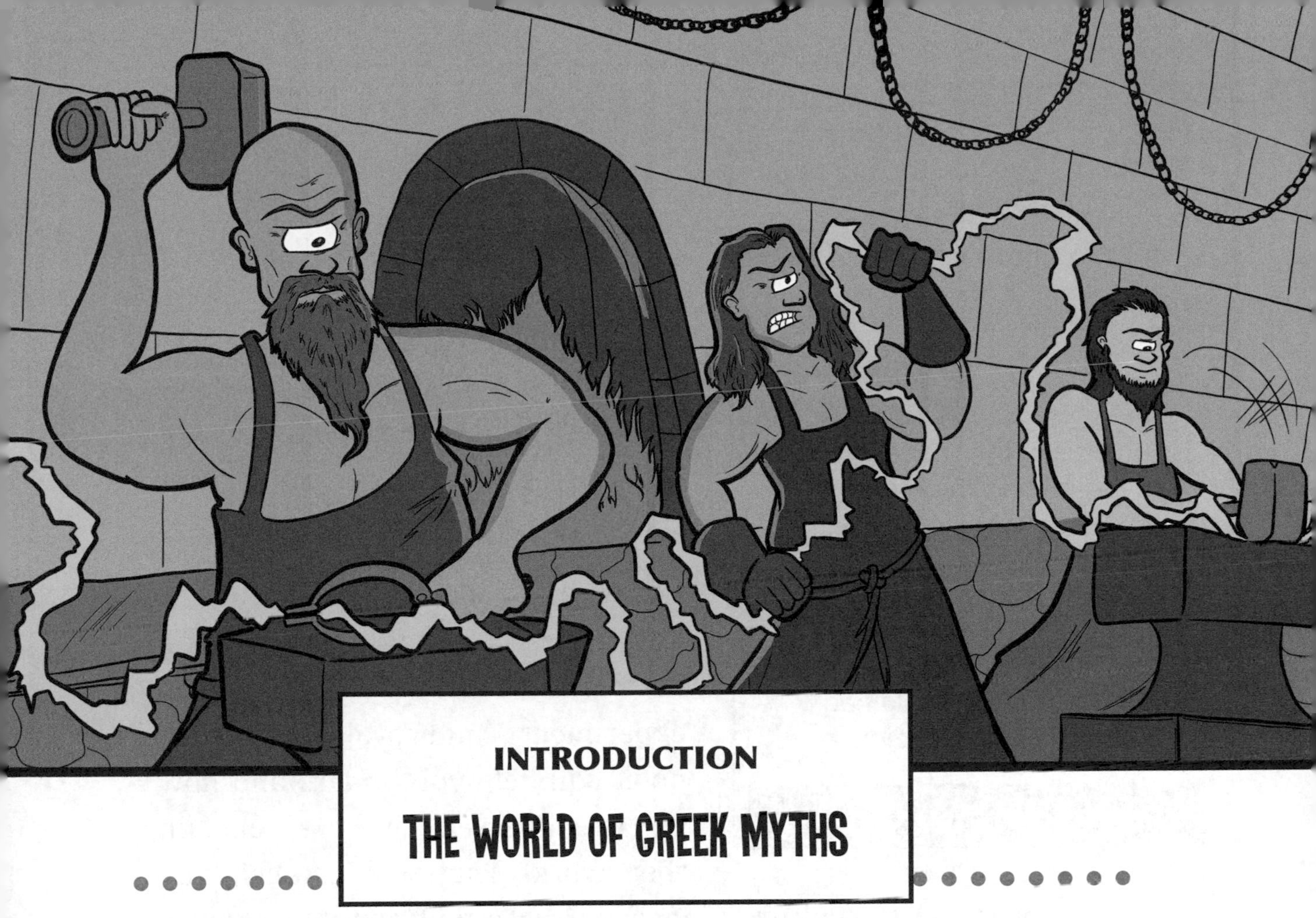

INTRODUCTION

THE WORLD OF GREEK MYTHS

Imagine a world filled with gods and goddesses, heroes and heroines. In this world, there are battles for control of the universe. There are awesome adventures in labyrinths and one-eyed monsters forging thunderbolts. What is this incredible land? It is the world of Greek myths, stories that express the beliefs of the ancient Greek people.

More than 3,000 years ago, the Greeks developed a rich culture. Have you watched the Olympics? Have you looked through a telescope at a group of stars in the shape of a warrior called Orion? Have you been to the theater or studied our democratic government? All of these things come from ancient Greece!

WORDS TO KNOW

myth: a traditional story that expresses the beliefs and values of a group of people.

culture: the beliefs and way of life of a group of people.

Explore Greek Myths! will take you on a journey from Mount Olympus to the underworld. You will read myths about King Midas, Medusa, and the Trojan Horse. You'll discover the daring adventures of heroes such as Heracles and Odysseus.

Learning about Greek myths also means learning about science, astronomy, and geography. The experiments and projects in this book will help you understand how the Greeks used myths to explain their world. They will also help you discover how the culture of ancient Greece continues to influence our world today.

WORDS TO KNOW

Mount Olympus: the home of the Greek gods.

astronomy: the study of the sun, moon, stars, planets, and space.

geography: the study of the earth and its features, especially the shape of the land and the effect of human activity on the earth.

pantheon: a group of gods belonging to a religion.

supernatural: something that cannot be explained using the laws of science.

WHAT ARE MYTHS?

Have you ever wondered why the earth shakes or why we have seasons? The ancient Greeks wondered about these things, too. But science could not yet provide them with answers. They created stories called myths with a pantheon of gods and other supernatural creatures to explain natural events.

Many of the names in this book are hard to say, but you can hear them spoken online. Go to Merriam-Webster.com, search for the word, and press the 🔊 symbol next to your word to hear it spoken.

KEYWORD PROMPTS

The Greeks added gods and goddesses to every part of their lives. No matter who you were in Greek society, from a noble to a thief, there was a god for you. The 12 greatest gods were the Olympians and they lived on Mount Olympus.

society: an organized community of people with shared laws, traditions, and values.

prophecy: a prediction of the future.

WORDS TO KNOW

Gods looked and acted like people. Unlike people, the Greek gods had superpowers and lived forever without growing old. No one had X-ray vision, but there were gods who could control the air, land, and sea. Zeus was the most important god. He ruled over the heavens and the earth.

SYMBOLS OF THE GODS

When ancient Greeks painted, drew, and sculpted the gods and goddesses, they used different symbols for each one so viewers would know who was who! Here are some of the symbols of the ancient gods and goddesses.

Zeus: king of the gods who rules over the earth and the heavens

Hera: queen of the gods and goddess of women and marriage

Apollo: god of the sun, music, and prophecy

Artemis: goddess of the hunt

Athena: goddess of wisdom and war

Aphrodite: goddess of love

Ares: god of war

Poseidon: god of the sea

Demeter: goddess of grain

Hermes: god of travel and language

Dionysus: god of wine and revelry

Hades: god of the underworld and death

WORDS TO KNOW

BCE: put after a date, BCE stands for Before Common Era and counts down to zero. CE stands for Common Era and counts up from zero. These nonreligious terms correspond to BC and AD. This book was printed in 2016 CE.

ode: a poem set to music that celebrates a person, place, or thing.

phenomenon: something seen or observed.

altar: a raised table used for religious purposes.

votive: a small offering to the gods, such as a coin.

offering: an object given to the gods as a gift.

sacrifice: an offering of an animal to the gods.

Pindar was a great Greek poet. Around 500 BCE, Pindar wrote poems set to music, called odes. Some of his best-known odes celebrated athletic superstars. He compared them to mythical heroes.

HONORING THE GODS

Religion was an important part of everyday Greek life. The Greeks told many myths about the gods and how they caused natural phenomenon. They prayed to the gods and asked for their support because they believed that the gods could help them. The Greeks also believed that the gods could make a person's life miserable. If you thought gods were that powerful, wouldn't you want to keep them happy? The Greeks did!

They worshiped the gods at altars in the courtyards of their homes and temples. The Greeks left votives at their altars, including small coins and statues. They made offerings to the gods, such as wine, milk, and honey mixed with water. They sacrificed animals, including goats and pigs. They built temples for the gods and worshiped them with religious festivals during the year.

The ancient Olympic Games were even another way the Greeks worshiped the gods. These games were part of a five-day religious festival to honor Zeus. During the games, thousands of athletes came to Olympia from all over Greece to compete. But no girls were allowed on the field! Competitions were only for men.

WORDS TO KNOW

Olympic Games: a global sporting event held every two years. In ancient Greece, these events took place every four years in Olympia, Greece, in honor of Zeus.

700 BCE - ATHENS

2012 CE - BEIJING

Athletes prayed to the gods for success. On the third day of the festival, priests sacrificed 100 oxen to honor Zeus at his grand temple. Inside the temple was an amazing treasure. It was a 42-foot-high statue of Zeus, covered in ivory and gold, by the sculptor Phidias. Zeus is said to have sent a lightning bolt to strike the ground near the statue to show his approval.

Do you watch today's Olympic Games? How are they different from the ancient games? How are they similar?

WORDS TO KNOW

epic: a long story that celebrates the adventures and achievements of a god or hero in verse.

TELLING MYTHS

The Greeks told myths through storytelling. If you were a kid back then, you might have heard a traveling poet, or bard, tell a myth. Bards memorized myths and recited them as they went from town to town to earn money. Myths were not written down until much later.

Do you know the story about the slow tortoise who beat the fast hare in a race? It is a fable recorded by Aesop, a storyteller in ancient Greece. *Aesop's Fables* used animals to teach people lessons.

Around 750 BCE, the Greeks adopted an alphabet from the Phoenicians. You'll read more about the Phoenicians later in this book. With an alphabet, the Greeks could write myths down. Two of the earliest sources for myths are the epic poems *The Iliad* and *The Odyssey.* They tell of the gods and goddesses, the Trojan War, and the hero Odysseus's 10-year journey home. His trip should have taken only weeks!

Many people believe that the Greek poet Homer composed these epics. Stories tell us that Homer was a blind storyteller. But some researchers believe that several wandering poets wrote the poems. We might never know which answer is correct.

KNOW YOUR MYTHS!

THE GODS CREATE THE HEAVENS AND EARTH

In the beginning, there was a shapeless darkness called Chaos. After Chaos came Gaia the Earth, Tartarus, a pit deep within Earth, and Eros, love. From Gaia came Uranus, the sky. They became parents to one-eyed giants called Cyclops, 100-handed Giants, and the powerful **Titans**. But Uranus hated the sight of the Cyclops and the Giants. Fearing their power, he threw them into a dark pit within Earth.

Gaia wanted her children to be free. She helped her son, Cronus, the bravest of all the Titans, destroy Uranus and become king. But Cronus was afraid that one of his children might kill him. Each time his wife, Rhea, gave birth, he swallowed the child. When Rhea was about to give birth to her sixth child, Zeus, she tricked her husband. Rhea gave Cronus a stone to swallow wrapped in a blanket. The real baby, Zeus, was safe on the island of Crete.

When Zeus grew up, he forced his father to throw up his sisters and brothers, including Hestia, Demeter, Hera, Hades, and Poseidon. Together, the siblings fought Cronus and won. When the battle was over, Zeus and his brothers divided the world. Hades became ruler of the underworld. Poseidon became the god of the sea. Zeus would rule the heavens and the earth.

Hesiod is another important ancient poet. Around 700 BCE, he wrote the epics *Theogony* and *Works and Days. Theogony* explained how the world was created. *Works and Days* provided the Greeks with practical information about their daily lives, such as how to run a farm.

In *Explore Greek Myths!*, you'll explore the culture, geography, technology, language, and arts of ancient Greece through their myths. Let's start our journey!

WORDS TO KNOW

Titans: the first family on Earth.

GOOD STUDY PRACTICES

Every good mythologist keeps a study journal! A mythologist is a person who studies myths. Choose a notebook to use as your study journal. Write down your ideas, observations, and comparisons as you read this book.

Each chapter of this book begins with an essential question to help guide your exploration of Greek myths. Keep the question in your mind as you read the chapter. At the end of each chapter, use your study journal to record your thoughts and answers. Do your friends and classmates have different answers?

INVESTIGATE!

What are some characteristics of Greek myths?

Myth	Science
Greek myths say that Gaia the Earth, Tartarus, and Eros were created out of chaos, and from these three creatures came all the gods and goddesses.	Scientists believe that the earth was created during huge collisions of energy billions of years ago. We are still learning how life evolved on this planet.

As you learn about Greek myths, use your study journal to compare and contrast the mythical explanations of the ancient Greeks with the scientific explanations we use today. You'll do projects to explore the real science behind natural events such as earthquakes and whirlpools.

Keep track of your observations and ideas. Are there any similarities between myths and real science? How are they different? Do people use myths and stories today to explain things we don't understand?

SUPPLIES

- white poster board
- pencil
- ruler
- crayons
- colored pens
- scissors

PROJECT!

GREEK GODS MEMORY GAME

Greek gods and goddesses were linked to symbols or objects that reflected their interests and personalities. Many had more than one symbol. In this game, you will design one playing card for each god and goddess and one for their corresponding symbols. You can use images of the gods and their symbols within this book for reference or ask an adult to help you find images online.

1 Using the ruler and pencil, create a grid of 24 squares on the poster board. A common size for playing cards is 2½ by 3½ inches, but you can adjust the size.

2 Draw one god on each card. Draw the god's symbols on another card.

3 Cut out each card. Now you are ready to play the game! Ask a friend to play this game with you or play alone.

4 Place the cards in rows, face down. Turn over a card and then select another. If the cards are a match, you can go again. If not, it is the other player's turn. Keep playing until all the cards are matched.

PROJECT!

MAKE A VOTIVE

The ancient Greeks used votives to honor the gods. You can make your own votive from tinfoil!

SUPPLIES

* tinfoil
* scissors
* water
* flour
* salt
* large mixing bowl
* newspaper
* paint or markers
* thin cardboard
* glue

1 To mold the foil into a small person representing you, begin by making two 4-inch slits at the top of the sheet of foil, 2½ inches in from each side. Make another 4-inch slit at the bottom center of the foil. Make a short slit at the center of each side.

2 Take the middle piece at the top of the foil and scrunch it to form a head. Then, scrunch and bend the two side pieces for your arms. Repeat for the bottom pieces that will be your legs.

3 To make the papier mâché paste, pour one part flour to two parts water into a mixing bowl and add a sprinkle of salt. You will need about ½ cup of flour.

4 Rip the newspaper into long strips about 1 inch wide. Dip one strip at a time into the paste and wrap it around the sculpture. You should overlap the strips and completely cover the foil. Let it dry.

5 Add details to your sculpture with paint or markers. To create a base for your sculpture, cut out a square from the cardboard. Attach your sculpture to the base with glue.

THINK ABOUT IT: How could you make your sculpture appear to be moving?

PROJECT!

WRITE AN ODE

SUPPLIES

- study journal
- pencil

The ancient Greeks celebrated their gods with odes. Odes use similes, metaphors, and exaggeration. A simile uses words such as "like" or "as" to compare two things. A metaphor creates an image by comparing two very different things. An exaggeration is when you make a thing larger than it is. Try writing an ode to your lunch.

1 Pick one piece of food that you usually have for lunch. Write one sentence that praises your food. Talk to the food directly.

2 Using your five senses, write down adjectives that describe the food. Pick a few of these adjectives and write a sentence describing your food. Include a simile.

3 Write a sentence using a metaphor by comparing your food to something unusual. Write a sentence using exaggeration about your food.

4 Write one sentence that praises your food. Talk to the food directly. Now read your ode out loud.

An Ode to a Peanut Butter and Jelly Sandwich

Oh PB & J,

you are fast to make and better to eat.

You are a sticky treat with jelly like rubies.

You are the salt to my pepper and the cookie to my milk.

You are perfection in a jar.

Oh PB & J,

you are delicious morning, noon, and night.

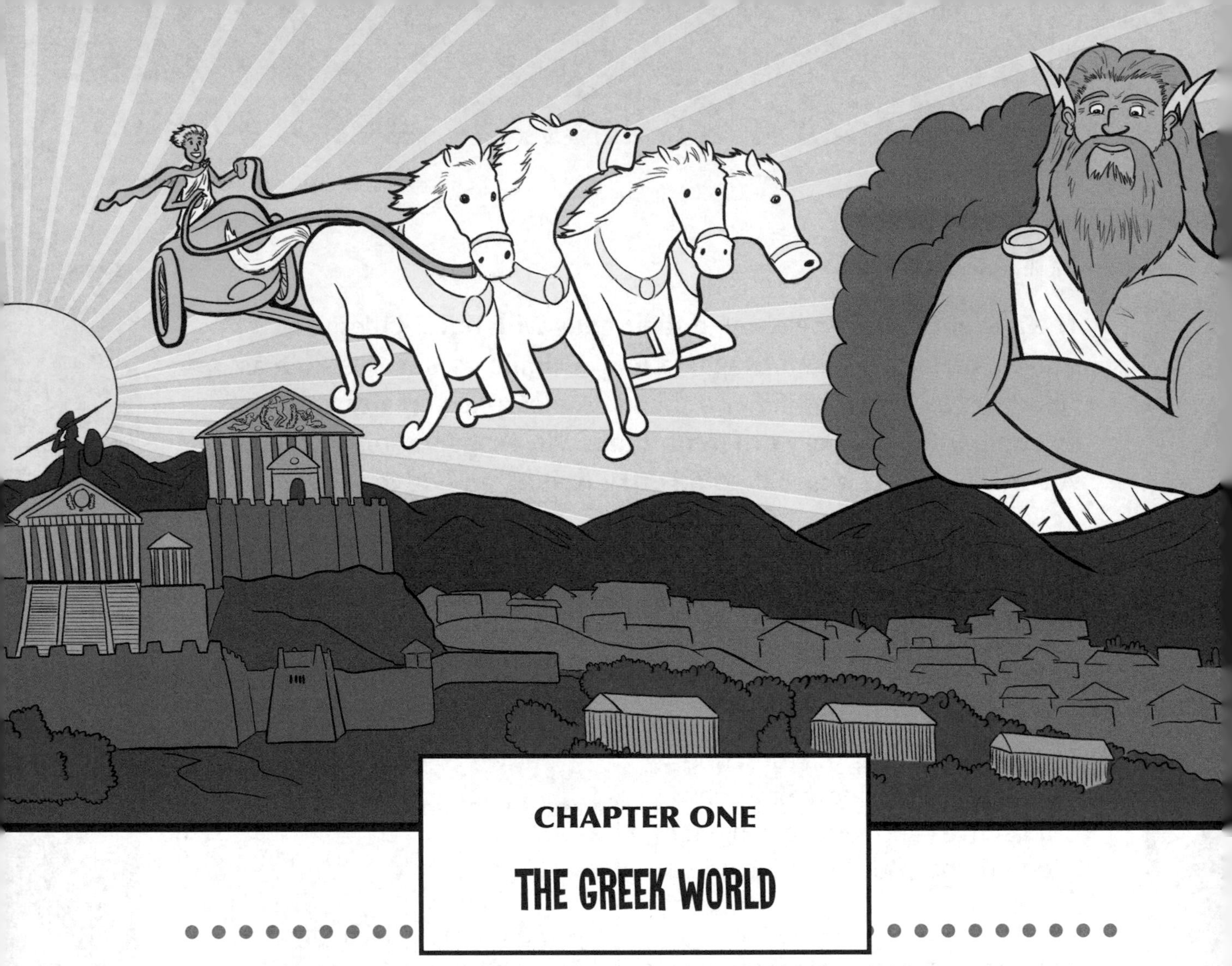

CHAPTER ONE

THE GREEK WORLD

Welcome to the homeland of the Hellenes! People who spoke Greek called themselves Hellenes and they called their homeland Hellas. It was the Romans who called them Greeks. In southern Italy, the Romans met a tribe of Greek-speaking people called the Graicoi. The Romans then used this name for all people who spoke Greek. The name stuck! Today, Greece is officially known as the Hellenic Republic.

The Greek homeland was in Southern Europe. It included thousands of islands in the Adriatic, Aegean, Black, Ionian, and Mediterranean Seas.

? INVESTIGATE!

Why did the Greeks use myths to explain natural disasters?

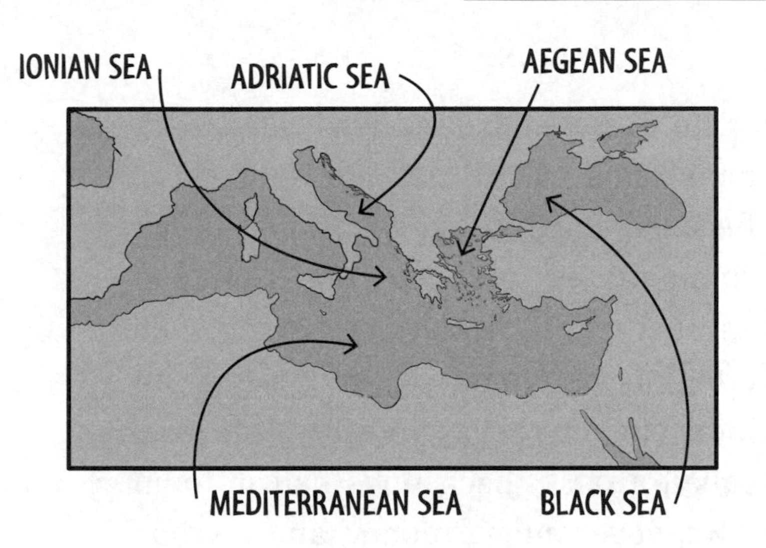

WORDS TO KNOW

plains: large, flat land areas.

The Greeks didn't know the science behind how land is formed and changed. They believed that a goddess named Gaia shaped the land, just as a potter shapes clay. In myths, Gaia pulled the earth up into mountains and flattened land into vast plains. Another creature, Uranus, helped create rivers and seas.

The Greeks told many more stories of gods who shaped their land. One story was about a war between the Titans, who were led by Atlas, and the Olympians, led by Zeus. After the war, Zeus punished Atlas for fighting against him by forcing the Titan to hold up the sky.

In another tale, the hero Perseus turned Atlas into stone using the head of a creature called Medusa. She had hissing snakes for hair! The body of Atlas became the Atlas Mountains of North Africa and his hair became the forests.

The Greek homeland was filled with mountains, rocky gorges, and cliffs. Because of this rugged land, Greek communities were cut off from one another. This isolation led to the creation of small city–states, or an independent society. A city–state was called a polis. Each polis had its own laws, government, money, and myths.

As people traded between city–states, myths spread from one area to another. Through many generations, Greek mythology adopted gods and goddesses from many different cultures around the Mediterranean Sea.

CITY-STATES

The city–states of Athens and Sparta became the largest and most important of Greece. Athens was a center for art and literature. Some of the most brilliant artists and philosophers lived there.

Democracy and the use of juries both appeared first in Athens. Jurors had to swear an oath to the gods Zeus, Apollo, and Demeter that they would uphold Athenian law. What do jurors swear on today?

WORDS TO KNOW

gorge: a narrow valley between hills or mountains, usually with steep rocky walls and a stream running through it.

polis: a Greek city–state.

literature: written work such as poems, plays, and novels.

philosopher: someone who thinks about and questions the way things are in the world.

democracy: a system of government where the people choose who will represent and govern them.

jury: a group of people, called jurors, who hear a case in court. Jurors give their opinion, called a verdict.

Anaximander (circa 610–546 BCE) was a great Greek philosopher and astronomer. He was the first Greek to create a map of the world. In the center of his map was Delphi. Zeus had declared Delphi the center of the world after his eagles collided over the city.

WORDS TO KNOW

circa: around that year. Abbreviated with a c (c.610–546 BCE).

Peloponnesus: the southern region of ancient Greece, where the Mycenaean civilization developed.

Persian Empire: a large empire to the south and east of Greece.

The Spartans were warriors. They created the strongest military in all of Greece. From the age of seven, Spartan boys left home to begin warrior training. Spartan girls were also expected to be physically strong so they would have healthy babies.

The Athenians and the Spartans did not always get along. From 431 BCE to 404 BCE, they fought a 27-year war called the Peloponnesian War. However, they did join forces to fight off invaders from the Persian Empire.

DAYS, NIGHTS, AND WEATHER

The ancient Greeks used myths to explain how the day changed to night and back again. If you asked them about the sun or the moon, they might have told you about three Titan siblings: Eos, Helios, and Selene.

discus: a circular disc that was thrown by athletes in ancient Greece and by the god Apollo.

WORDS TO KNOW

Eos was the goddess of the dawn. She made night vanish each morning when she woke. Her brother, Helios, the god of the sun, then charged out of his golden palace. Four magnificent horses with crowns of light pulled him across the sky. Once he reached the west, Helios disappeared into a golden cup and his other sister, Selene, the goddess of the moon, began to shine.

The Greeks also used myths to explain the weather. The four chief wind gods were Boreas (the North Wind), Zephyros (the West Wind), Notos (the South Wind), and Euros (the East Wind). Boreas brought winter. He swept down from the mountains blowing icy air over the land until Zephyros brought the spring breezes. Notos followed with summer storms and Euros blew the leaves off the trees in the fall.

In the story of Apollo and the Spartan prince, Hyacinthus, the West Wind Zephyros was jealous of their friendship. He caused Apollo's discus to strike Hyacinthus in the head, killing him. But the blood of Hyacinthus became the spring flower, hyacinth.

KNOW YOUR MYTHS!

THE STORY OF WINTER: HADES AND PERSEPHONE

Demeter is the goddess of grain and the harvest. Long ago, Demeter's beautiful daughter, Persephone, was kidnapped by her Uncle Hades, ruler of the Underworld. Demeter did not know what had happened to her daughter. She searched for her everywhere. Overcome with sadness, she promised that nothing would grow on Earth until her daughter was returned to her. The people begged the gods to help them. Zeus sent the messenger god, Hermes, to bring Persephone back.

During her time in the Underworld, Persephone refused to eat or drink, for she knew that anyone who did would be forced to remain there forever. But one day, she was overcome with hunger and ate four pomegranate seeds. This meant she had to live four months of each year with Hades. During this time we call winter, nothing grows on Earth. But Persephone spends the rest of the year with Demeter, and that is when the crops grow and the flowers bloom.

NATURAL DISASTERS

Greece lies in an area of the world where there are many earthquakes and an active chain of volcanoes. The people used their myths to explain these natural events.

Hephaestus was the Greek god of fire and metalworking. Some stories said that his forge was in the volcano on Lemnos Island in the Aegean Sea. Smoke or rumblings from the volcano were thought to be Hephaestus hard at work. According to Greek myth, he was creating amazing objects for the gods, such as the helmet of Hermes.

WORDS TO KNOW

forge: a furnace where metal is heated up to make tools or other objects.

demi-god: a person with one parent who is human and one parent who is a god.

WORDS TO KNOW

THEN & NOW

THEN: Around 360 BCE, the Greek philosopher Plato wrote about a city called Atlantis that was founded by **demi-gods**. It was a beautiful city that suddenly disappeared under water.

NOW: Some researchers believe that Atlantis was a real place. One possible site is an island near Crete. In 1646 BCE, a huge volcanic eruption blew out the interior of the island.

A far more dangerous creature lived under a more active volcano called Mount Etna. Typhon was a giant so huge that his head reached the stars. Typhon's anger was said to cause fountains of lava to hiss and pour from the volcano.

The Greeks also told stories to explain the shaking ground of earthquakes and the uncontrollable seas of storms. When Poseidon was angry, he caused the waters to surge and the ground to shake.

INVESTIGATE!

It's time to consider and discuss the Essential Question: Why did the Greeks use myths to explain natural disasters?

PROJECT!

EXPERIMENT WITH EARTHQUAKES

SUPPLIES

- shoe box
- scissors
- string
- 5–7 paper clips

Today, we know that earthquakes are caused by tectonic plates moving below the surface of the earth. In this experiment, you will learn how earthquake waves travel through solid objects. Are there any similarities between the ancient Greek myths and the science we know today?

Caution: Have an adult help with poking holes in the box.

1 Take the lid from the box and set it to one side. Stand the box on end. Make a hole in the top center of the box with the scissors. Make another hole directly beneath this on the bottom of the box.

2 Thread the string through the holes and secure each end with tape. Evenly space out the paper clips on the string. The number of paper clips depends on the size of your box.

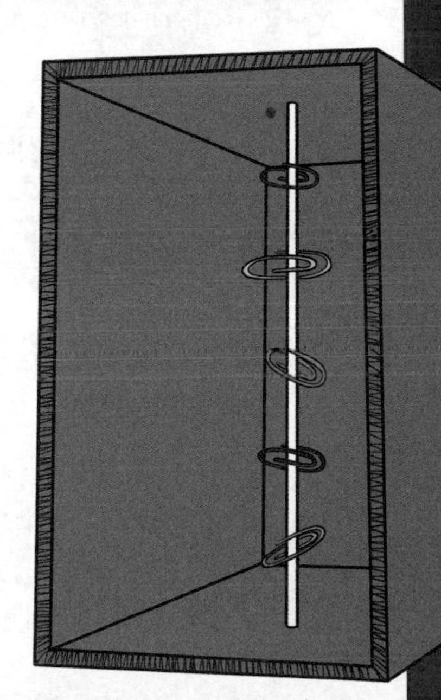

3 Place your box on a table. Give the table a little shake and observe what happens to your paper clips.

TRY THIS! Place your box on different surfaces. Strike each surface and observe what happens to the paper clips. What do you think will happen if you use different thicknesses of string or different sizes of paper clips?

WORDS TO KNOW

tectonic plates: large slabs of the earth's crust that are in constant motion. The plates move on the hot, melted layer of earth below.

PROJECT!

MAKE A MAP OF ANCIENT GREECE

Make a topographical map of ancient Greece with cookie dough. This kind of map shows the features of the land, such as mountains and gorges.

Caution: Have an adult help with cutting and baking.

SUPPLIES

* computer with Internet access and a printer
* paper
* scissors
* tube of sugar cookie dough
* rolling pin
* circular baking pan
* plastic knife
* baking chips, sprinkles, colored sugars, icing pens

1 Print out the Ancient Greece map template from nomadpress.net/projects/templates or copy the map on the next page. Cut out the four sections and set aside.

2 Roll out the cookie dough according to instructions.

3 Place your largest paper piece on top of the dough first. Cut around the shape with the knife. Place the piece on the baking pan with central and northern Greece at the top.

4 Repeat step three for Peloponnesus, Asia Minor, and Crete. Asia Minor will on the right side of the pan and Crete at the bottom.

5 Add baking chips to your map to represent Greece's mountains. Mold the long coastline with your fingers.

6 Follow the instructions on the package and bake your map. When the map has cooled completely, add more details with the sprinkles and icing pens.

PROJECT!

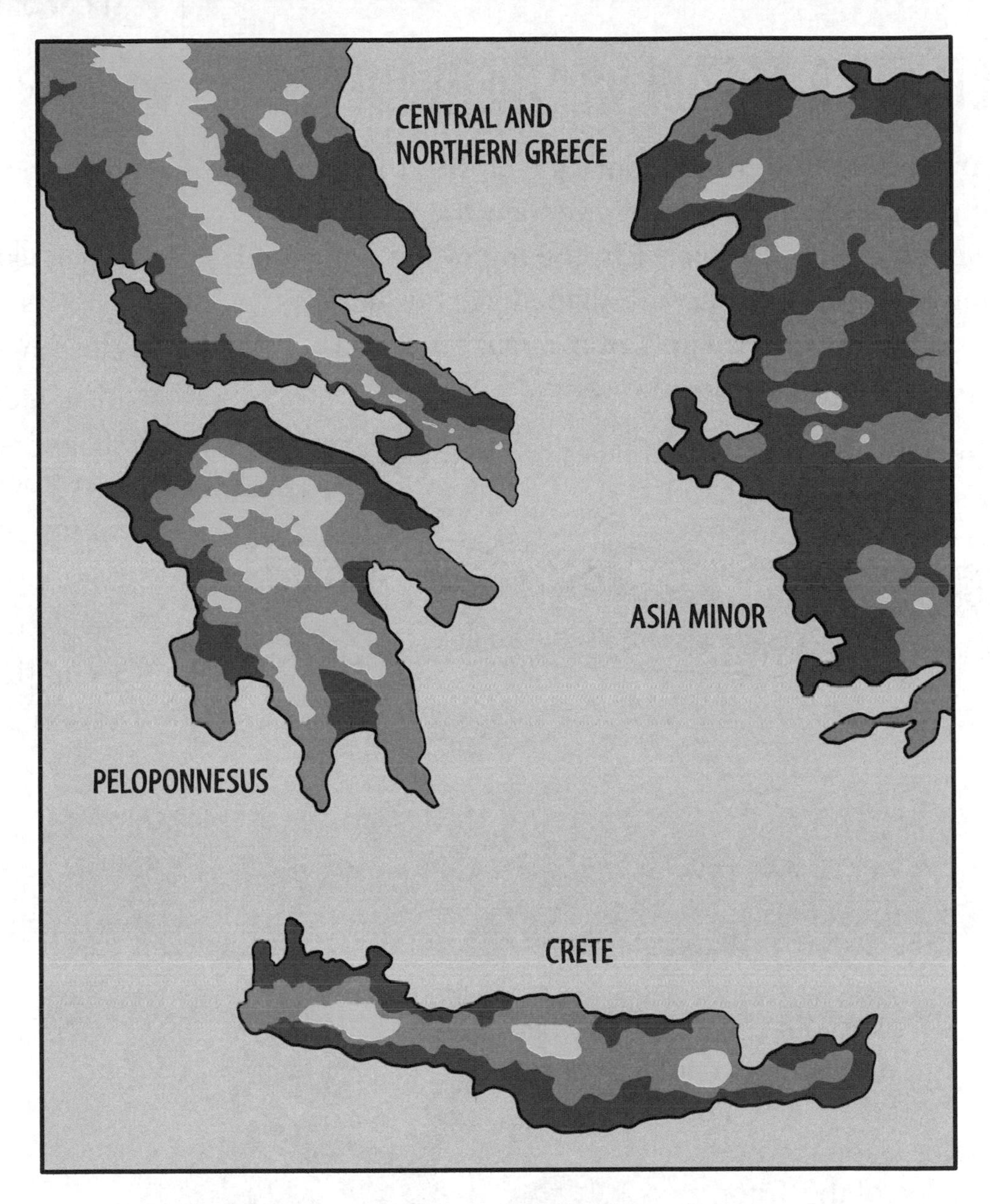

THINK ABOUT IT: Do you live in an area that is flat or has mountains? How does the geography around you affect the way you live? Do you think it would have been different in the ancient past, when there were no cars?

PROJECT!

CREATE A TRITON WEATHERVANE

Around 50 BCE, the Athenians built the Tower of the Winds to show which direction the wind gods were blowing the wind. On the top of the octagonal tower was a weathervane shaped like Poseidon's son, Triton, a merman. You can make a Triton weathervane to study the wind.

To learn more and see images of the tower, visit this website.

KEYWORD PROMPTS

ancient technology ingenious invention

SUPPLIES

* sheet of white paper
* colored pens and pencils
* recycled greeting card
* white glue
* scissors
* clear tape
* long wide straw
* sheet of colored construction paper
* narrow straw
* bamboo skewer
* small bead
* 1 cup rice
* mason jar

1 Looking at the example, draw a Triton about 5 by 7 inches on the white paper.

2 Color your drawing and glue it to the greeting card to make it sturdier. When dry, cut it out. Tape the bottom edge of the Triton to the length of the wide straw.

PROJECT!

3 Draw an arrowhead and a tail on the yellow construction paper. Cut these pieces out and tape them to opposite ends of the wide straw.

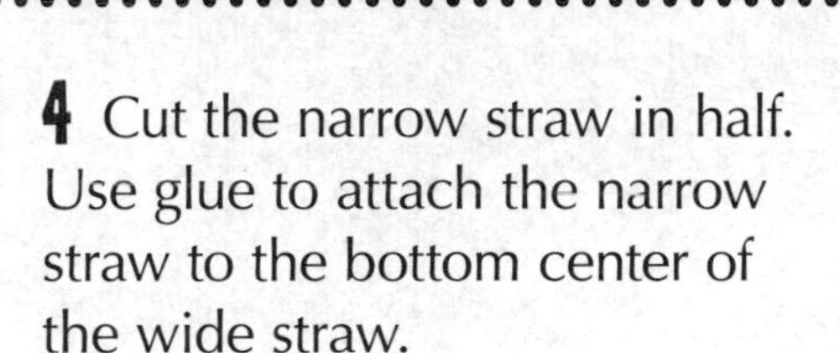

4 Cut the narrow straw in half. Use glue to attach the narrow straw to the bottom center of the wide straw.

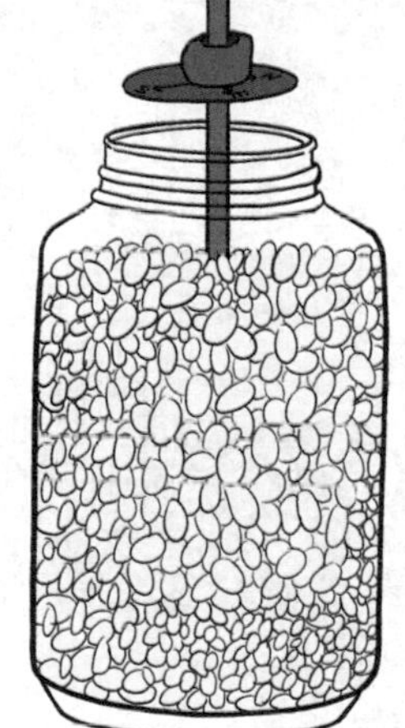

5 Next, draw a circle with a 2-inch diameter. Cut it out and draw the four compass points on it—N, S, E, W. This is a **compass rose**.

6 Push the skewer through the center of the paper compass. Push the compass three-quarters of the way up the stick. Slide a small bead down the skewer so it rests on the compass. Next, slide the top of the skewer into the narrow straw. Set to one side.

7 Fill the mason jar with rice. Stick your weathervane in the middle of the jar. Take it outside and observe how it works.

TRY THIS! Observe the wind during several days and at different times. Which way does it blow? Record your results.

WORDS TO KNOW

compass rose: a circle drawn on a map to show north, south, east, and west.

CHAPTER TWO

MONSTERS AND MAYHEM

Do you like scary movies? Boys and girls in ancient Greece did not have scary movies to watch, but there were stories that could scare their togas off! Myths were full of monsters, curses, and badly behaved gods. There were horrible creatures with rows of sharp teeth and mile-long tentacles. Some monsters were a patchwork of different animals, such as the Chimera. It had the body of a lion, the head of a goat, and the tail of a snake.

INVESTIGATE!

Do stories told today contain lessons? Can you think of examples?

Some myths were told to teach lessons. Monsters represented evil and chaos. They did not behave as the Greeks believed people should. Monsters, unlike heroes, were not brave, noble, or honorable. Monsters sometimes ate people!

Often, the gods used monsters to punish people. Sometimes, they changed people into monsters. When the Greeks heard these myths, they learned that it was never wise to be proud, greedy, or vain.

toga: a loose, one-piece garment worn by men in ancient Greece and ancient Rome.

curse: words that people believe cause harm.

chaos: a state of complete confusion.

civilization: a community of people that is advanced in art, science, and government.

WORDS TO KNOW

MINOANS AND A MAZE

The first advanced civilization to develop in the Aegean Sea was the Minoan civilization on the island of Crete. The Minoans farmed olives and made beautiful pottery decorated with dolphins and starfish. They built huge palaces up to five stories high.

ATHENA AND ARACHNE

Athena was the goddess of wisdom, the arts, and war. She once turned a girl named Arachne into a spider because Arachne claimed that she was a better weaver than the goddess.

You can listen to the myth and see artwork that shows the story at this website.

KEYWORD PROMPTS

voyage with gods Athena Arachne

archaeologist: a scientist who studies ancient people through the objects they left behind.

WORDS TO KNOW

An archaeologist named Sir Arthur Evans (1851–1941) named the Minoans after a mythical king called Minos. King Minos was said to have built a maze to contain a beast called the Minotaur.

In 1900, Sir Arthur Evans began excavating the ruins of a palace at Knossos in Crete. His team discovered hundreds of maze-like rooms surrounding a large central courtyard. No one is certain why the palace was built like this. The Minoans may have used some of the rooms as workshops or private apartments. The confusing pattern of rooms, staircases, and corridors may have led to stories about a mysterious maze.

WHAT DID POSEIDON SAY TO THE SEA MONSTER?

What's Kraken?

THE MONSTER FAMILY

Some of the most famous Greek monsters were the children of Typhon and Echidna, a half-woman, half-snake monster. Their children were monstrous! Their offspring included the Hydra, the Chimera, the Sphinx, and Cerberus.

immortal: describes a person who cannot die.

fresco: a painting made on fresh, wet plaster.

WORDS TO KNOW

The Hydra terrorized the people of Lerna. The hideous serpent had nine heads, including one that was immortal and had fangs dripping with poison. The great hero Heracles, along with his nephew, Iolaus, came to rid the town of the serpent. Heracles crushed the heads with his club. No sooner had he destroyed one than two heads grew in its place! When Iolaus saw this, he held a torch to each stump and stopped new heads from forming. Then Heracles chopped off the immortal head and buried it. What lesson does this story teach?

THE MINOAN FRESCOES

When Sir Arthur Evans excavated the Minoan site, he discovered beautiful pictures called frescoes on the walls. They show Minoans leaping over the horns of bulls like gymnasts.

You can see the frescoes at this website.

KEYWORD PROMPTS

ancient history Minoan fresco

KNOW YOUR MYTHS!

THESEUS AND THE MINOTAUR

Poseidon gave a beautiful white bull to King Minos. The bull was so beautiful that the king decided that he would not sacrifice it to the god. Angered, Poseidon make the king's wife fall in love with the bull. She gave birth to a monster, the Minotaur. It was part human and part bull. King Minos's architect, Daedalus, built a maze to hold it.

Every nine years, the Minotaur devoured seven young men and women who were sent to it as sacrifices. The Athenian hero Theseus vowed that he would stop this custom. When Theseus landed on the island, King Minos's daughter, Ariadne, fell in love with him. Ariadne gave Theseus a sword and a ball of thread. Theseus unwound the thread as he crept through the maze. In its center, he found the Minotaur and drove his sword through him. Theseus rescued the young men and women. They all escaped by following the thread.

The Sphinx was a clever monster with the face of a woman, wings, and the body of a lion. She lived near Thebes in central Greece. She loved to play games, but they were not fun for her victims. She would kidnap people from Thebes and only let them go if they could answer a riddle. But they never could. So she ate them! The King of Thebes offered to give up his crown to anyone who could outwit the Sphinx.

One day, Oedipus came to Thebes. He offered to answer the riddle of the Sphinx. Oedipus picked his way to her lair over the bones of her victims. When the Sphinx saw him, she asked him this riddle: "What walks on four legs in the morning, two legs in the afternoon, and three legs in the evening?"

WORDS TO KNOW

riddle: a puzzle that is asked as a question.

Oedipus guessed that it was a person, because a person crawls as a baby, walks as an adult, and uses a cane when old. The Sphinx hated to lose and threw herself off a cliff.

VANITY

Narcissism is a word that describes people who are very selfish. The word comes from a story about a boy called Narcissus. He was the son of a river god and a water spirit. One day, a girl named Echo fell in love with him, but Narcissus ignored her. Poor Echo faded away until only her voice was left.

The goddess Nemesis cursed Narcissus by making him fall in love with his reflection in a lake. He stayed by the lake until he starved to death. What was this story teaching about narcissism?

The Strait of Messina in the Mediterranean Sea was said to be guarded by the monsters Charybdis and Scylla. Charybdis had a whirlpool for a mouth that could swallow boats whole! Scylla enjoyed feasting on sailors with her razor-sharp teeth.

WORDS TO KNOW

narcissism: the feeling of being overly interested in your own appearance.

Another vain character was Medusa, the most beautiful girl in Greece. She boasted about her looks. The goddess Athena overheard Medusa and punished her. Athena turned Medusa's hair into a mass of slithering snakes and gave Medusa a gaze that could turn a man to stone. Medusa was eventually killed by looking at her own reflection in Perseus's shield.

Why do you think these myths about vanity were told? What purpose might they have served in Greek society?

INVESTIGATE!

It's time to consider and discuss the Essential Question: Do stories told today contain lessons? Can you think of examples?

KNOW YOUR MYTHS!

THE GOLDEN WISH

One story from ancient Greece explained that there were more important things than money. Why is this a good lesson to learn?

King Midas loved money more than anything else. He asked the god Dionysus to make everything he touched turn to gold. Excited with his new power, the king turned flowers and leaves to gold. The king grabbed his daughter's hand to show her, but she too turned to gold! Everything he tried to eat and drink became gold. King Midas begged Dionysus to take the gift back. The god told him to bathe in the river Pactolus to wash away the magic.

PROJECT!

MAKE A LABYRINTH

Daedalus built a labyrinth for King Minos to contain a monster. You can create a small maze of your own, not for a Minotaur, but for a small marble. Will you be able to rescue the trapped marble?

SUPPLIES

* study journal and pencil
* shoebox lid
* wrapping paper
* scissors
* flexible straws
* glue
* marker
* marble

1 In your study journal, design and sketch a maze for your marble. Cover the outside of the shoebox lid with wrapping paper.

2 Create twists and turns in the box using straws. Cut the straws into different sizes and glue them in place. Make sure there is one path that goes all the way through.

3 Label one end of the maze "start" and the opposite end "finish."

4 Place your marble at the start. Try to roll the marble through the maze to the end. How hard is it? What can you do to make it harder?

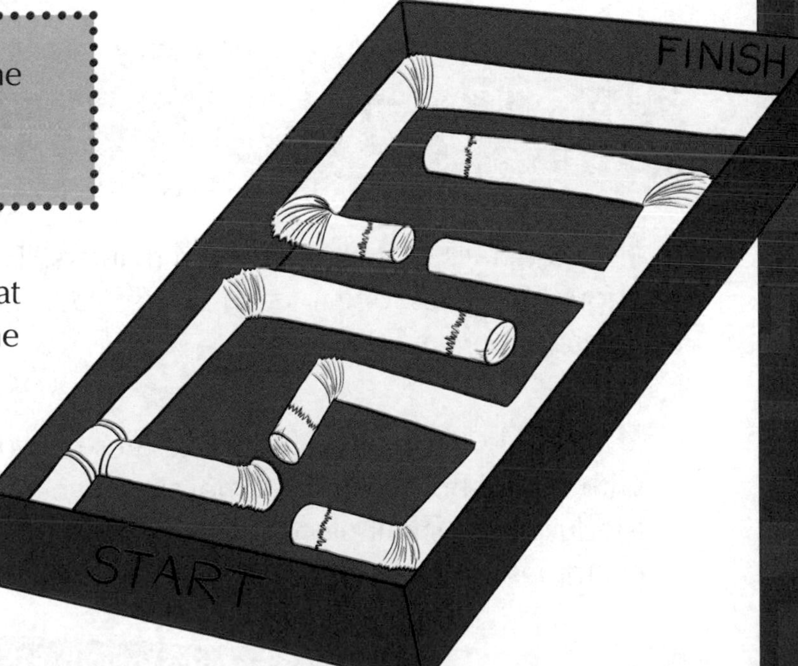

PROJECT!

MAKE A MEDUSA MASK

Medusa was a mythical monster that taught people lessons about vanity. How do we teach about vanity now? Create a Medusa mask by turning your handprints into two bunches of wriggling snakes. Who will your mask scare ?

SUPPLIES

* sheet of heavy green craft paper
* pencil
* scissors
* clear tape
* green paint
* sparkles
* paper plate
* paintbrush
* markers
* string

1 Spread your fingers out. Trace your hands on the paper, extending the line of each finger to turn them into wriggling snake heads. Cut the handprints out.

2 Tape the handprints together at the thumbs. Overlap the paper if the mask is too large for your face. Cut out eyeholes in the palm of each hand.

3 Mix paint with sparkles on a paper plate. Paint over the entire mask. Let it dry.

4 Add details to your mask with markers. Tape a piece of string about 12 inches long to each side of your mask. Now your mask is ready to wear.

TRY THIS! Greek artists made pictures called mosaics with tiny pebbles. Create a mosaic on your plate of Medusa with small pieces of paper and glue. See examples of a mosaic here.

KEYWORD PROMPTS

ancient technology ingenious invention

PROJECT!

DESIGN A MIDAS COIN

Around 600 BCE, the Greeks began making coins. Make a large gold coin inspired by King Midas.

SUPPLIES

* sheet of white paper
* small ceramic plate
* pencil
* textured objects
* yellow pencil or crayon
* metallic pen
* scissors

1 Place the plate on your paper and trace around it to make a circle. Set it to one side.

2 Look around your home or outside for objects that have a texture. What do you notice about the patterns or shapes of the objects you have collected?

3 To create an image on the circle, place it over one of the collected objects. Rub gently over the object with your yellow pencil or crayon. You can make your pattern more interesting by rubbing over more textures or by adding more detail with a metallic pen.

4 Cut out your large coin. Pin it to a bulletin board as a reminder of King Midas's story or punch a hole through the top, tie a string, and hang it up.

THINK ABOUT IT: Depending on where you are rubbing, does the color or texture vary? If so, why do you think this is?

Legend says that King Midas's swim in the river Pactolus to wash away the magic is why people once found gold along the river's banks.

PROJECT!

BUILD A WHIRLPOOL

Now we know that whirlpools are caused by ocean tides and currents moving in different directions. Why do you think ancient Greeks thought of them as the mouths of monsters? In this experiment, you can investigate the science behind whirlpools.

SUPPLIES

* two 2-liter plastic bottles
* water
* blue food coloring
* duct tape
* study journal and pencil
* scissors

Caution: Have an adult help with the scissors.

1 Rinse and clean the bottles. Fill one bottle three-quarters full with water. Add two drops of food coloring.

2 Seal the top of the bottle containing water with duct tape. Carefully make a small slit in the tape at the bottle's mouth with the pointy scissors. Repeat this step for the empty bottle.

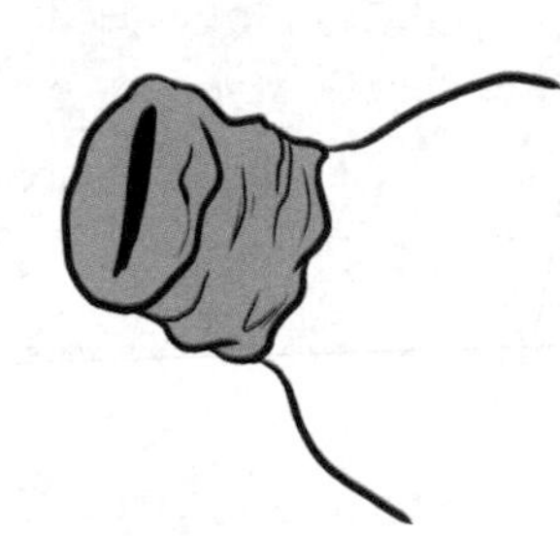

3 Place the opening of the empty bottle directly over the opening of the full bottle. Tape the two bottles together securely. You do not want any water to leak out.

WORDS TO KNOW

tide: the daily rise and fall of ocean water.

current: the steady flow of water or air in one direction.

PROJECT!

THEN & NOW

THEN: The Trojan Horse was a giant wooden horse built by the Greeks to take over Troy.

NOW: The Trojan Horse is a computer virus that sneaks into computers and spreads more viruses.

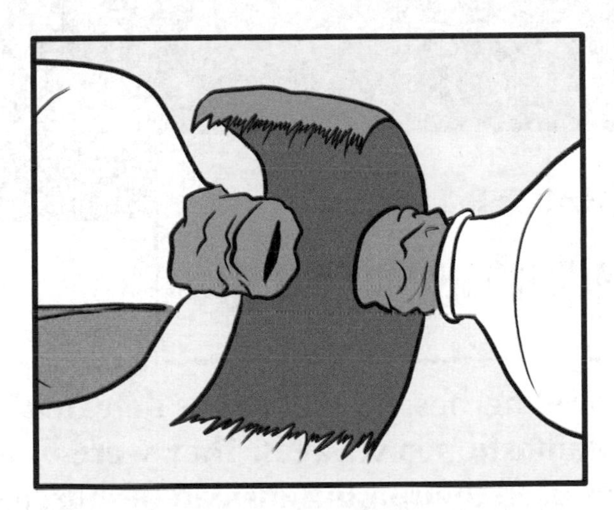

4 Flip the bottles so that the bottle containing water is on top. Swirl the bottles and observe what happens. Record your observations in your study journal.

THINK ABOUT IT: Does the speed at which you swirl the bottle affect the experiment? How? If you didn't swirl the bottles, what would happen? What would happen if you filled both bottles with water? Does the size of the slit affect the experiment?

CHAPTER THREE

HEROES AND IMPOSSIBLE TASKS

The ancient Greeks loved heroes. Greek heroes defeated monsters and set out on fantastic sea voyages. They were brave and strong. Some heroes used their brains instead of muscles to defeat evil. Some heroes had human parents and others were demi-gods. The Greeks built shrines to honor heroes. They worshiped them through sacrifices and offerings of food.

THE MYCENAEANS

Greeks believed that many of their legendary heroes lived during the Mycenaean Age. The Mycenaeans were the first people to speak a form of Greek. They lived on the southern peninsula of Greece, known as the Peloponnese.

INVESTIGATE!

Do Greek heroes share certain characteristics? Why?

From 1600 to 1100 BCE, Mycenae was the most powerful city-state on the Greek mainland. The Mycenaeans were traders and warriors. They built massive walls and gates to protect their cities. Some measured 40 feet high with stones that could weigh as much as 100 tons! Later, Greeks wondered if Giants had helped move these stones.

In the eleventh century, their fortified cities were invaded by the Dorians, a people from central Greece. The Mycenaean civilization disintegrated and Greece entered a Dark Age. This was a time when there was very little writing. Centuries later, a man named Homer spread stories about the feats and adventures of Mycenaean heroes and wars in *The Iliad* and *The Odyssey.*

shrine: a special, religious place.

Mycenaean Age: a Greek civilization that flourished from 1650 to 1200 BCE.

Dark Age: a time when a civilization undergoes a decline. The Dark Age in Greece lasted from 1100 to 700 BCE.

WORDS TO KNOW

One of the most famous stories was about the Trojan War. According to Homer, the Mycenaeans declared war on Troy. This city is in present-day Turkey. A beautiful woman named Helen was married to the Greek king, Menelaus of Sparta. But she ran away with Paris, a prince of Troy, and a great war began between the Greeks and the Trojans. Some researchers believe that Homer's story of the Trojan War was based on actual events.

KNOW YOUR MYTHS!

THE TROJAN WAR

According to myth, Eris, the goddess of discord, offered a golden apple to the fairest goddess. Hera, Athena, and Aphrodite chose a man called Paris to judge who was the fairest. Paris chose Aphrodite because she offered to make the beautiful Helen his wife. But Helen was already married to King Menelaus of Sparta. After Paris and Helen ran off to Troy, a great war began.

For 10 years, the Greeks could not get inside the thick walls that protected Troy. The gods helped both sides, but the city of Troy would not fall. Finally, a warrior named Odysseus devised a plan. He advised the Greeks to build a huge wooden horse. When it was completed, it was wheeled to the gates of Troy. The Greeks pretended to sail away. The people of Troy opened the city's gates and wheeled in the horse, thinking it a gift. But inside the horse was a group of Greek warriors. At night, the Greek soldiers came out and took over the city!

MEET THE HEROES

Achilles was a Greek hero in the Trojan War. When Achilles was a baby, his mother was told that he would die at a young age. Determined that no harm would ever come to him, she held him by the heel and bathed him in the River Styx, which ran between the earth and the underworld. Water from the river was said to make a person immortal.

Achilles grew up to be a great soldier. During the Trojan War, the god Apollo told Paris of Achilles's weakness. Since his mother had held Achilles by the heel when she bathed him, his heel was not protected. Paris struck Achilles on his heel with a poisoned arrow and killed him. Today, we use the expression "Achilles's heel" to describe a person's weakness.

THEN & NOW

THEN: Heracles was a favorite subject of Greek and later Roman artists. His likeness appeared in frescos and sculptures.

NOW: In 1997, Disney reimagined Heracles as a good-natured hero who must save the universe from Hades.

You might know Heracles better by his Roman name, Hercules. He wasn't perfect and often his bad temper got him into trouble, but he always tried to correct his mistakes. Heracles's father was Zeus, and his human mother was Alcmene. Zeus's wife, Hera, hated Heracles. She cast a spell and made him go insane. During this time, Heracles accidently killed his family.

When the spell was lifted, Heracles was overcome with grief. He performed 12 difficult labors to show how sorry he was for killing his family. He battled monsters and stole man-eating horses from a giant. After 12 long years, Heracles finished the labors. Only then could he forgive himself for his crime. When Heracles died, Zeus made him immortal.

WHERE DO GREEK WOMEN GET HAIRCUTS?

At a Hera salon!

SOCRATES

Socrates (469–399 BCE) was a great Greek teacher who taught people to question everything, even the gods. His ideas angered some Athenians, and they brought him to trial. The jury found him guilty of mocking the gods and sentenced him to death.

You can read the words of Socrates, written down by his student, Plato.

KEYWORD PROMPTS

Illinois Socrates Plato

Atalanta was a famous female hero. Stories say that her father left her as a baby in a forest because he had wanted a boy. But a group of hunters found Atalanta and looked after her. She became a strong athlete and a fierce warrior. Her family wanted her to marry, but she did not. Atalanta swore that she would only marry a man who could beat her in a footrace. Many men tried, but all failed.

A young man named Melanion raced her. He threw three golden apples in front of Atalanta as they raced. She could not resist picking them up, which allowed Melanion to win.

Sadly, the couple did not live happily ever after. The god Zeus became angry with them and turned them into lions!

INVESTIGATE!

It's time to consider and discuss the Essential Question: Do Greek heroes share certain characteristics? Why?

PROJECT!

BE A GREEK SHIP BUILDER

The ancient Greeks built many types of ships that relied on wind and oar power. *The Iliad* describes Odysseus's ship as being fast and black. Odysseus's ship may have been a long and narrow ship called a penteconter that was used for trade and warfare. In this activity, you are going to create sails for a ship to see how the design affects the ship's performance.

Caution: Ask an adult to help you cut the juice carton.

SUPPLIES

- 2-quart empty juice carton
- scissors
- masking tape
- colored markers
- craft paper
- study journal
- pencil
- skewers
- clear tape
- large plastic container
- stopwatch

1 Cut the juice container in half lengthwise. Cover the container with masking tape.

2 On the ship's bow, draw an "evil eye" with the markers. Greek sailors thought that the eye would keep the ship safe from harm. Set the ship to one side.

3 From the craft paper, cut out shapes to try as sails. Cut triangles, rectangles, and squares in various sizes. Before you begin the experiment, write down in your study journal which geometric shape and size you think will propel your ship the fastest and why.

4 Use one shape at a time. Tape the shape to a skewer. Secure the skewer to the middle of the ship with tape.

PROJECT!

5 Fill the large container with water. Place your ship at one end. Blow on the ship's sail and time how long it takes for it to reach the opposite side. Repeat this step with all the shapes. What do you learn from your experiment?

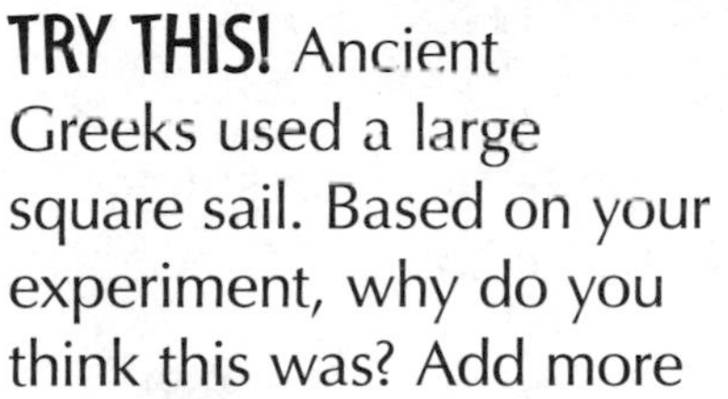

TRY THIS! Ancient Greeks used a large square sail. Based on your experiment, why do you think this was? Add more than one sail to your ship and see if this affects your results. You can also try making sails from different materials.

THE *ARGO*

In the myth *The Golden Fleece*, a hero named Jason sails a strong ship across the Black Sea to find the mythical fleece of the Golden Ram. The goddess Athena helps the craftsman Argus build Jason's ship, the *Argo*. Athena carves a magical figurehead for the *Argo* from a sacred oak tree. The figurehead can talk and predict the future.

PROJECT!

GO GO ODYSSEUS BOARD GAME

Design an adventure board game. The object of the game is to get the hero Odysseus safely back to his home in Ithaca. To play the game, invite a friend and roll the die. The highest roll goes first. Follow the directions on each square.

SUPPLIES

- 5 different colors of craft paper
- poster board
- pencil
- ruler
- glue stick
- markers
- coins for tokens
- die

1 Cut out five squares of paper from each color and arrange the 25 squares into a path on the poster board. Glue them into place.

2 Write one of the sentences on the next page on each square. Think of additional challenges for Odysseus for the last five squares.

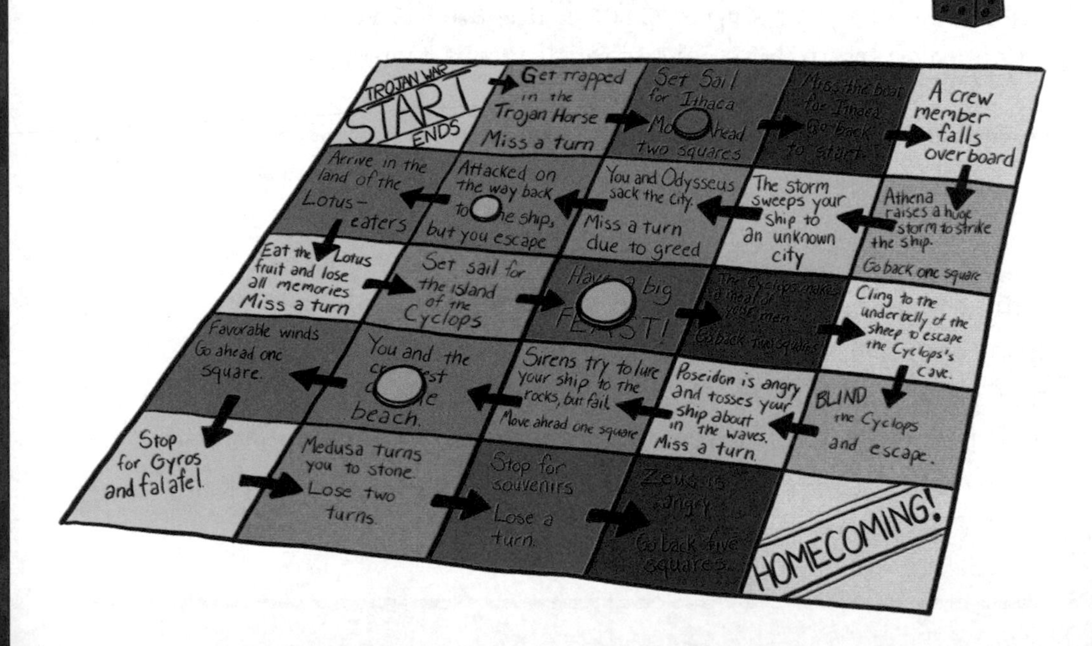

PROJECT!

Start. The 10-year war against the Trojans is over.

Get trapped in the Trojan Horse! Miss a turn.

Set sail for Ithaca. Move ahead two squares.

Miss the boat for Ithaca. Go back to start.

A crew member falls overboard.

Athena raises a huge storm to strike the ship. Go back one square.

The storm sweeps your ship to an unknown city.

You and Odysseus sack the city. Miss a turn due to greed.

Attacked on the way back to the ship, but you escape.

Arrive in the land of the Lotus-eaters.

Eat the Lotus fruit and lose all memories. Miss a turn.

Set sail for the island of the Cyclops.

Have a big feast!

The Cyclops makes a meal of two of your men. Go back two squares.

Cling onto the underbelly of the sheep to escape the Cyclops's cave.

Blind the Cyclops and escape.

Poseidon is angry and tosses your ship about in the waves. Miss a turn.

Sirens try to lure your ship onto the rocks, but fail. Move ahead one square.

You and the crew rest on a beach.

Create more adventures for Odysseus. The last square will be his homecoming!

PROJECT!

SEND A MESSAGE FROM TROY

SUPPLIES

- paper
- pencil
- 2 flashlights

The Greeks used beacons to send messages over long distances. The Greek poet Aeschylus wrote that beacons were used to alert the Greeks that Troy had fallen. In this activity, you are going to use flashlights to send a message to a friend.

1 Write out the alphabet on the piece of paper.

2 Decide how many flashes and the length of each flash that will represent each letter. For example, you may choose one short flash to represent the letter A, one short and one long flash for the letter B, and so on. You can also try using two flashlights to represent a letter.

3 After you have created your code, share a copy of it with a friend.

4 Write down a short message and then flash the message to your friend.

THINK ABOUT IT: Today, we use light to send messages through email and texting. What are some of the differences between the ways the ancient Greeks used light and the way we use light to communicate?

PROJECT!

MAKE A LYRE

Some ancient Greek poets created music with a lyre and set their words to song. A lyre is a small instrument like a harp. Make an instrument and compose a song using the sound waves created by your lyre strings.

SUPPLIES

* shoebox lid
* protractor
* scissors
* paper plate
* paint
* sponge
* glue
* 4 elastic bands in various sizes
* toilet paper roll

1 Three-quarters of the way down the box lid, use your protractor to make a circle with a 3-inch diameter. Poke your scissors in and cut it out.

2 Pour a few paint colors onto the paper plate. Dip your sponge into the paint and add color to your box lid. Let the box dry.

3 Using the scissors, poke four evenly spaced holes on both short sides of the lid.

4 Cut each elastic band. Tie one end of an elastic to a hole. Then stretch it across the lyre to its corresponding hole on the other side and knot. Use all four bands in this way.

5 Cut the toilet paper roll to fit in the instrument. Slide one piece under the elastics to raise them. Try to play a song on your lyre.

TRY THIS! Sound is produced by vibration. When you pluck the elastics they vibrate and make a sound. What happens to the sound if you use elastics of different thicknesses? Try moving the toilet paper roll up and down. Does this affect the sound?

CHAPTER FOUR

GODS AND GRANDEUR

The Greeks were great architects and builders. While the Greeks built simple homes out of clay bricks and wood beams, their public buildings, including stadiums and theaters, were grand. There are examples of these beautiful buildings throughout Greece.

The Greeks developed rules for building to achieve harmony and balance. These rules included how many columns a building should have and what those columns should look like. Later, these rules became known as three styles of architecture—Doric, Ionic, and Corinthian.

> **INVESTIGATE!**
>
> How did the ancient Greeks build such impressive structures without modern machinery?

The Doric was the oldest style, with sturdy-looking columns. The Ionic style was much more graceful and decorative. At the top of Ionic columns were swirls like snail shells. The Corinthian columns were the most elaborate, with curling leaves.

Architects all over the world have been inspired by Greek monuments and buildings. The Brandenburg Gate in Berlin, Germany, was inspired by the gateway to the temples on the Acropolis in Athens. The U.S. Capitol in Washington, DC, has tall Ionic columns. Under the roof of the main entrance is a pediment, just like one you would find on a Greek temple.

Plato was a great Greek philosopher who founded a school near Athens in 380 BCE. One of Plato's ideas was that only beautiful buildings should be built in Greece.

WORDS TO KNOW

harmony: the arrangement of parts in pleasing relation to each other.

Doric: a style of architecture featuring simple columns topped by squares.

Ionic: a style of architecture featuring slender columns with scroll-like details at the top.

Corinthian: a style of architecture featuring decorative columns with leaves, flowers, and scrolls.

Acropolis: a rocky ledge high above Athens, home to ancient buildings, including the Parthenon.

pediment: the triangular piece on the front of some buildings at the top.

patron: a person or supernatural being that is believed to support and protect a person, group, or place.

trident: a spear with three sharp points.

WORDS TO KNOW

THE PARTHENON

Some of the most impressive Greek structures were temples. These were built to honor the gods. Temples also showed the power and prestige of powerful city–states, such as Athens.

Originally, the kings of Athens built fine palaces at the summit of a huge rock at the center of Athens, called the Acropolis. The word *acropolis* means "city at the top." But none of those palaces of the Acropolis survive today.

KNOW YOUR MYTHS!

THE CONTEST FOR ATHENS

A long time ago, there was a king who was half snake and half man. He was called King Cecrops. King Cecrops ruled over a city that was so magnificent that both Athena and Poseidon wanted to be its patron. Athena, being wise, suggested a contest to see which god could give the city the best present. King Cecrops would be the judge.

A huge crowd gathered at the Acropolis to see what magnificent gifts the gods would give their city. Athena made an olive tree grow. The people could eat its fruit and use its oil. When it was Poseidon's turn, he struck the ground with his trident, causing a magnificent sea to burst from the ground. The people rushed to drink the water, but they discovered that it was salty. It was decided that Athena's gift was more useful, and she was named the patron of Athens.

The Athenians built the Parthenon to honor the city's protector, Athena. The temple was massive! The base of the Parthenon was half the length of a football field.

Inside the Parthenon was a huge statue of Athena made of ivory and more than 2,500 pounds of gold. A long frieze wrapped around the top of the inner chamber. It showed the gods and people enjoying an Athenian festival.

WORDS TO KNOW

frieze: a carved band of stone or marble that often tells a story or shows characters from a myth.

pulley: a wheel with a groove for a rope used to lift a load.

lever: a bar that is used to lift a heavy load.

mortar: a building material that hardens when it dries. It is used like glue to hold bricks and stones together.

quarry: a pit where stone is cut for building.

The Athenians built the Parthenon in eight years, between 447 and 432 BCE. Imagine the work it took to build this structure without modern machinery. They used simple machines, such as pulleys and levers, to construct the Parthenon. The Greeks were such expert builders that the blocks fit together perfectly with no need for mortar. Metal clamps made the structure stronger.

The marble for the project came from a quarry more than 11 miles away. Wagons brought the marble up the steep slopes of the Acropolis. How might this differ from a modern construction zone?

orchestra: a stage where Greek singers, actors, and musicians acted out the drama in a play.

WORDS TO KNOW

THEATERS

In addition to temples, the Greeks built stadiums, baths, and long covered walkways called stoas. These were arranged around a market square. The Greeks also built large outdoor theaters on hillsides to take advantage of the natural slope. You can still see and sit in some of them today!

In the sixth century BCE, the Athenians built the Theatre of Dionysus. Dionysus was the god of wine and the patron of the arts. Some historians believe that the first play was staged at this theater in 530 BCE. An actor, Thespis, wrote the play. From his name comes the English word *thespian*, which means "actor."

The Theatre of Dionysus was massive. It could sit 17,000 people! Audiences sat in semi-circular rows of benches carved into the hillside above. Important people, such as government officials and priests, sat in the front row. Actors were lowered onto the round stage, called an orchestra, astride horses or in chariots. The theater used a system of pulleys for these special effects.

The ancient Greeks held festivals for the gods. The Athenians were especially busy with their religious festivals. They had one nearly every three days. Their most important festival was the Panathenaia. It honored their patron goddess, Athena.

INVESTIGATE!

It's time to consider and discuss the Essential Question: How did the ancient Greeks build such impressive structures without modern machinery?

PROJECT!

EXPERIMENT WITH PULLEYS

The ancient Greeks used pulleys in theaters during performances and to help them build large buildings. We still use pulleys today! Try this activity to see a simple pulley in action.

Caution: Have an adult help you poke the hole in the box.

SUPPLIES

* wooden skewer
* shoebox
* empty spool
* string
* scissors
* sheet of paper
* coloring pencils
* small objects to lift
* clear tape

1 Push the skewer through the top edge of the box. Leave enough of the skewer poking out to then thread it through the spool. Your spool needs to be able to rotate freely.

2 Cut a piece of string about 24 inches in length and knot the ends. Place around the spool. This is your fixed pulley.

3 On the paper, design a small flag for your pulley to lift. It should be about 1 by 2 inches. Use a small piece of clear tape to attach your flag to the string. How can you position your pulley to raise or lower your flag?

TRY THIS! Try making a moveable pulley that moves freely up or down. Cut a yard of string. Tape one end to the edge of a table. Loop the string around the spool. Pull on the free end to make the pulley move. To lift a weight with this pulley, wrap one end of a paper clip around the spool and make a hook to grab something to lift. Try adding another spool to your string to make a compound pulley and record your findings. What happens? Can you lift a heavier load?

WORDS TO KNOW

compound pulley: a system of fixed and movable pulleys that work together.

PROJECT!

EXPERIMENT WITH LEVERS

Greek mathematician and inventor Archimedes was the first person to write about using a lever. A lever rests on a pivot, or a fulcrum. When you push on the bar, your force moves the lever, which moves the load. In this experiment, you will move the fulcrum and observe what happens.

SUPPLIES

- ruler
- eraser
- baking cups
- clear tape
- small weights such as coins paper clips, buttons
- pencil
- study journal

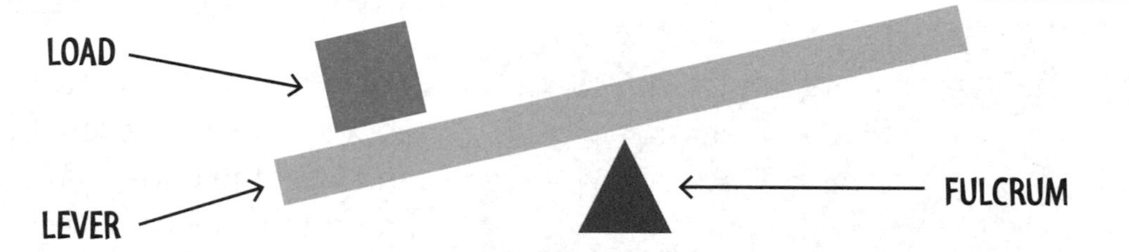

1 Rest the ruler on an eraser. Tape the baking cup to one end of the ruler. Place one of your weights in the cup.

2 Use your fingers to apply pressure to one end of the ruler. What happens? Write down your observations in your study journal.

WORDS TO KNOW

pivot: the center on which something turns or balances.

PROJECT!

3 Experiment with moving the fulcrum. First try moving it closer to the weight and then try moving it farther away from the weight. What do you observe?

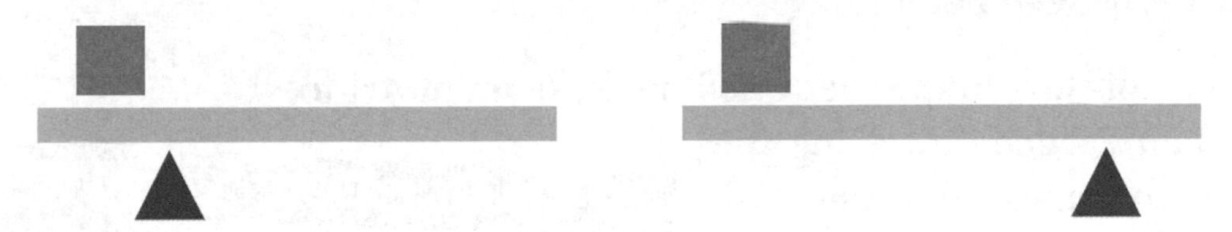

4 Repeat the experiment with different weights and make notes of any differences in your results.

THINK ABOUT IT: How does moving the load closer or farther from the fulcrum affect the experiment? In which direction does the load move when effort is applied to the ruler? What other simple machines might builders in ancient Greece have used?

LEVERS IN EVERYDAY LIFE

Just like the ancient Greeks, you use levers every day to help you do work. A pair of scissors is an example of a first-class lever. The fulcrum is in the middle, where the two blades connect, and the effort and load are at opposite ends. There are many other levers all over your home. A stapler, for example, is a second-class lever. The fulcrum and effort are at opposite ends, and the load is in the middle. What are some other levers you use?

PROJECT!

DESIGN A GREEK COLUMN

SUPPLIES

- ✱ study journal and pencil
- ✱ sheet of white paper
- ✱ ruler
- ✱ modeling clay
- ✱ paper towel roll
- ✱ paint

Imagine that you have been asked by the city of Athens to help design their next temple. As a test of your skill, you need to design a column that no one has ever seen before.

Visit this link to the Metropolitan Museum of Art to watch a video describing the differences between the three different styles of Greek columns.

KEYWORD PROMPTS

MET Greek architecture

1 In your mythology journal, design your column. Draw the basic silhouette of a column with the ruler. Think about the three styles of Greek columns. Decide which elements you are going to use. Draw the base of your column. Will the top of your column be the same as your base?

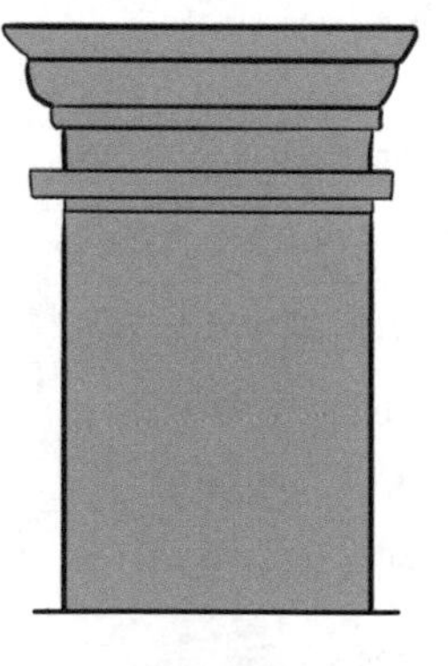

DORIC

IONIC

CORINTHIAN

PROJECT!

2 Before adding details to your column, answer the following questions. What type of building will your column be used for? If it is part of a temple, which god or goddess will it be for? Will you incorporate symbols connected to the gods?

3 Tear off a piece of clay for the base of your column. Mold it into the shape you want and attach it to the paper towel roll by pressing the clay around the roll. Repeat this step for the top of your column.

4 Allow the clay pieces to dry. Add additional details to your column with the clay and paint it.

THINK ABOUT IT: What public or private buildings where you live use columns? Are the columns holding up parts of the building or are they just for decoration? How can you tell?

THEN & NOW

THEN: Ancient Greeks cut and polished the columns on the Parthenon by hand. They were twice as fast as modern craftsmen because they drew on centuries of knowledge.

NOW: Restorers working on the Parthenon's columns use a machine to carve the fluted designs in fresh marble. Small details are still done by hand.

PROJECT!

MAKE A MODEL OF THE PARTHENON

The Parthenon remains one of the most popular tourist attractions in all of Greece. Though most of the sculptures are gone, people can still marvel at the size of its columns. Create a model to see how it was designed.

SUPPLIES

- 2 flattened cereal boxes
- pencil
- ruler
- scissors
- newspaper
- white paint
- paintbrush
- white glue or masking tape
- paper
- colored pens (optional)

1 Cut out the base and the roof of your Parthenon from a cereal box. Both pieces should measure 8½ by 11 inches.

2 Cut out eight columns for the front measuring about ½ inch in width by 11 inches in height. Make more columns for the sides. The actual Parthenon has 17 columns along each side, but you may want to adjust this number. The back of your temple will be open so that you can design the interior.

Many sculptures from the Parthenon are now housed in the British Museum in London. You can see these sculptures here. Why do you think it's important to preserve pieces of ancient artwork? What might audiences today learn from them?

KEYWORD PROMPTS

British Museum Greece sculpture video

PS

PROJECT!

3 Spread newspaper over a flat surface. Arrange your Parthenon pieces on top. Paint all the pieces white. Let them dry before painting the other side.

4 Glue or tape the base of each column to the base of the temple. Apply glue to the edges of the roof. Lay it on top of the columns. Press gently to secure the roof.

5 Cut out a large triangle for the front of your temple. Use the pencils to draw a frieze on it. Tape the bottom edge of the triangle to the top of the roof.

TRY THIS! Use paint to add details to your temple. Greek temples are white today because the original paint colors wore away. What colors do you think the Greeks painted with?

CHAPTER FIVE

ANCIENT GREECE IN TODAY'S WORLD!

Writers, architects, filmmakers, and musicians have all been inspired by Greek gods and goddesses, monsters, and heroes. Greek myths have been reinvented as modern dance, ballet, and opera. They have inspired popular book series and lovable characters. Movies, television shows, and manga all use magical creatures from Greek mythology.

Ancient Greece has also influenced medicine, philosophy, math, and science. Today, doctors swear the Hippocratic Oath, named after the ancient Greek doctor Hippocrates (c.470–377 BCE.) Unlike other physicians of his time, Hippocrates did not believe that the gods were responsible for a person's illness. Instead, he argued that illness was caused by something natural.

INVESTIGATE!

How is the civilization of ancient Greece important today?

ASTRONOMY

The names of many of the planets come from Greek or Roman mythology. They are based on how the planets move and how they appear from Earth. These planet names include Venus, Uranus, and Mercury.

The 12 signs of the zodiac and the constellations also have their origins in Greek myths. Aries represents the Ram with the Golden Fleece that Jason wanted. Leo is the lion that Heracles killed. Scorpius is the scorpion that killed the hero Orion. Two of the brightest stars in Gemini were the twins Pollux and Castor, whom the Greeks worshiped as though they were gods.

WORDS TO KNOW

manga: a style of comic book from Japan.

zodiac: the 12 sections in the sky that ancient astronomers used to describe the path of the sun.

constellation: a group of stars in the sky that resembles a certain shape, such as the Big Dipper. There are 88 official constellations in the sky.

PYTHAGORAS

Pythagoras (580–500 BCE) was a great Greek philosopher and mathematician. He advised his students, who were called Pythagoreans, to use reasoning to solve problems. He discovered that the three interior angles of a triangle always equal 180 degrees.

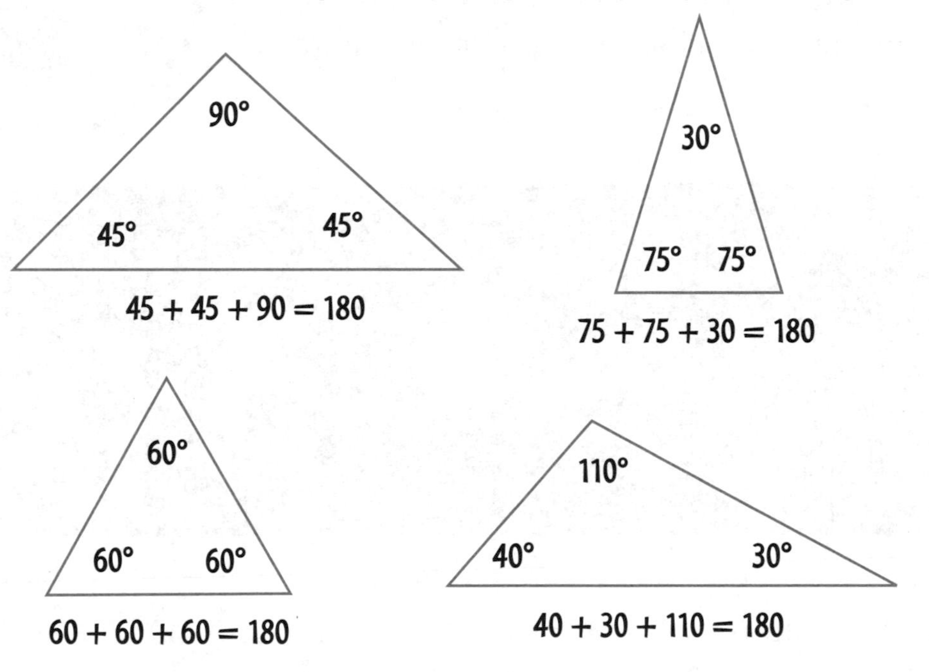

MOVIES AND BOOKS

Have you read books or seen movies based on Greek myths? Disney has animated centaurs, sirens, and Greek gods, though often the characters are different from the original myths. For example, in the film *The Little Mermaid,* the ruler of the sea is called Triton instead of Poseidon. In Greek mythology, Triton was the son of Poseidon. Triton was able to calm the seas by blowing on a conch shell.

satyr: a mythical creature that is half man and half goat.

WORDS TO KNOW

In 1997, Disney made an animation about Heracles but used the Roman spelling, Hercules, for the god's name. Disney's Hercules had a satyr called Phil for a personal trainer and launched the Titans into outer space.

Japanese manga artists have been adapting Greek myths for decades. The manga *Knights of the Zodiac (Saint Seiya)* shows Athena and her knights fighting other Olympian gods who want to take over the earth. The Knights are a group of young people with special powers who have sworn to protect the goddess.

In 1960, NASA began working on an exciting project to land people on the moon. The project needed a name. While reading a book on mythology, the director of research, Dr. Abe Silverstein, saw an image of Apollo. In 1969, *Apollo 11* became the first flight to land people on the moon.

The most successful movie franchise to date was based on author Rick Riordan's *Percy Jackson and the Olympians* books. Two movies have been made so far: *Percy Jackson & the Olympians: The Lightning Thief* and *Percy Jackson: Sea of Monsters*.

oracle: a spiritual advisor believed to be able to predict the future.

WORDS TO KNOW

KNOW YOUR MYTHS!

PERSEUS AND ANDROMEDA

The hero Perseus was the son of Zeus and Danae, a mortal woman. In one famous story, Perseus rescued Princess Andromeda.

Andromeda's parents boasted that she was prettier than everyone, even the daughters of Poseidon. When the god heard this, he sent a sea monster to destroy their kingdom. An **oracle** advised the parents to sacrifice Andromeda to the sea monster. They chained Andromeda to a cliff by the sea. Perseus, who had just killed Medusa, happened to fly by. He turned the sea monster to stone by pulling Medusa's head out of a bag. Perseus freed Andromeda and they married. The Greeks believed that the couple became constellations after they died. Can you find them in the sky? Have an adult help you!

SPORTS AND ADVERTISING

Today, businesses have found new ways to draw comparisons to the gods and heroes of Greek mythology. Sports teams are often named after heroic characters in Greek myths. Popular names include the Spartans, Tritons, and Argonauts. Why do you think they do this?

Myths are an important source of inspiration for companies selling all kinds of products, from beverages to clothing. These companies include the Olympus camera company, Trident gum, and Orion Pictures. Can you name a large sporting company that begins with the letter N? Nike was the winged goddess of victory and associated with speed, strength, and victory.

IT IS ALL GREEK TO ME

Many of the words we use today can be traced back to Greek words. *Democracy* comes from the Greek word *demokratia,* meaning "people and power." *Ostracize* is from the Greek verb *ostrakizein*. The Athenians had a system called ostracism that was used to get rid of citizens who were unpopular. To get a citizen exiled from the city, someone had to write their name on a piece of clay pottery called an ostrakon. If 6,000 people voted for the same person, that person was kicked out of Athens for 10 years. Do you think this was fair?

WORDS TO KNOW

ostracism: being excluded from a group.

citizen: a person who has all the rights and responsibilities that come with being a full member of a country. In Athens, only adult males could be citizens.

exiled: forced to leave one's country.

Town founders have also found inspiration in mythology. Athens is not only the capital of Greece, but a city in more than 12 American states, including Georgia.

Some letters in our English alphabet came to us from the Greeks. Around 750 BCE, the Greeks developed a writing system. It was based on an alphabet from a group of people called the Phoenicians, who lived in the eastern Mediterranean. The Greek alphabet ended up being 24 letters.

boustrophedon: a system of writing on alternate lines and in opposite directions.

furrow: a long, narrow trail in the soil.

WORDS TO KNOW

THEN & NOW

THEN: More than 2,400 years ago, the first democracy in the world began in Athens. All free Athenian adult males could vote, but women or slaves could not vote.

NOW: The Hellenic Republic is a republic. This means the Greek people hold the power and elect representatives who form a government.

During the development of their language, the Greeks created a form of writing called boustrophedon, or ox-turning. In this style of writing, each line changes direction just as an ox turns at the end of a furrow. There are no spaces between words, the letters are all capitals, and the letters are reversed or mirrored every other row. By the seventh century BCE, the Greeks found writing from left to right easier.

THEFOLLOWING
FOELPMASASI
BOUSTROPHEDON
GNINRUT-XORO

The Greek alphabet is still being used in Greece. We also use Greek letters to stand for symbols in mathematics and science.

INVESTIGATE!

It's time to consider and discuss the Essential Question:
How is the civilization of ancient Greece important today?

PROJECT!

CONSTELLATION KEY CHAIN

The ancient Greeks looked at the stars and connected them to characters in stories. You can create Greek constellation patterns on cards.

SUPPLIES

- mug
- pencil
- flattened cereal box
- scissors
- pin
- hole punch
- key ring

1 Trace around the mug on the cereal box six times. Cut out the circles.

KEYWORD PROMPTS

Greek constellations

2 Look at this website for Greek constellations for your circles. Draw one constellation per circle.

3 Use the pin to poke a hole through each star in the constellation. Write the name of the constellation at the bottom.

4 Place the circles in a pile and punch a hole through the top of each card. Open the key ring and push one end through each of the holes. Close the key ring by pushing the ends together.

5 In a dim room, hold one card up at a time to a light source. What do you see?

THINK ABOUT IT: Which constellation has the greatest number of stars? Which has the least amount of stars? Different cultures saw different things in the constellations. Why do you think this was?

PROJECT!

DESIGN A HEROIC SPACECRAFT

Imagine that NASA has hired you as a designer for an exciting new program to explore space. Your first assignment is to design a new spacecraft based on the strengths of one character from a Greek myth.

SUPPLIES

* study journal and pencil
* scrap paper
* boxes of various sizes
* white glue
* masking tape
* acrylic paint
* sponge or brush
* crayons and markers
* craft paper
* decorations (buttons, pompoms, glitter, foam)

1 Answer the following questions before you begin to build. Write your answers in your mythology journal. Look at your answers as you build your spacecraft.

- **Who?**
  Will computers or astronauts run the spacecraft?
- **What?**
  What is the purpose of the mission? For example, is it to bring back samples, conduct experiments, or search for new life forms?
- **When?**
  How long will the mission be?
- **Where?**
  Choose a planet or moon in our solar system. Will your spacecraft study the planet from space or will it move over the surface of the planet?
- **Why?**
  Why does the character from Greek mythology best represent your mission?

PROJECT!

2 Choose items from the craft supply list to build your spacecraft. Look through your recycling box for more empty containers.

3 Before adding an item, think about its purpose. What does your final design look like? How does it reflect the Greek hero you chose?

THINK ABOUT IT: Many Greek heroes face challenges on their journeys. NASA astronauts also encounter problems on space missions that they need to solve. Think about difficulties your spacecraft might encounter. How would you solve these problems? Could they be solved from Earth or on the spacecraft?

PROJECT!

CREATE A STORYBOARD

SUPPLIES

- scrap paper
- pen
- sheet of poster board
- ruler
- pencil
- colored pencils and markers

Create a storyboard based on your favorite Greek myth. The challenge will be to tell the story in only six squares. See if your friends can correctly guess the myth.

1 On a piece of scrap paper, brainstorm your myth. Think about six major events from the myth. Be certain to write down the major characters and the setting.

2 On a large sheet of poster board, draw six large squares for your storyboard.

3 Draw one major event in each box. Add words to support the drawings.

4 Read over your storyboard. Does it tell the whole myth? Add details or change the event. When you are happy with your storyboard, add color to each square.

5 Display your storyboard. See if your friends can guess the myth.

PROJECT!

IT'S ALL GREEK TO ME!

SUPPLIES

- study journal
- pencil
- colored pencils

Create a message for a friend using boustrophedon. Your message will have no punctuation, all capital letters, alternating lines, and reversed lettering, or mirroring.

1 Write a simple message with three sentences on a piece of paper. The more sentences you add, the more challenging your message will be.

2 To rewrite your message using boustrophedon, use only capital letters and leave out all punctuation and gaps between the words. You will also need to alternate the direction of each line and reverse the lettering. See the example below. Use a mirror to help!

3 Give your message to a friend. Can they read it?

PEGASUSWASA
ESROHDEGNIW
INGREEKMYTHOLOGY
SUSAGEPDENRUTSUEZ
INTOACONSTELLATION
DEIDEHNEHW

CHAPTER SIX

SIMILAR STORIES

Does Greek mythology remind you of stories from other cultures? There are similar stories from around the world. In 336 BCE, Alexander, the son of King Philip II of Macedon, conquered Greece and much of Asia with his powerful army. As he traveled, he spread Greek culture, including Greek art and medicine.

INVESTIGATE!

Why do cultures tell similar stories to explain events people don't understand?

Norse: people from Denmark, Norway, and Sweden.

WORDS TO KNOW

Similar themes and characters to Greek myths appear in many other world myths and legends. Yet, many of these cultures had no contact with ancient Greece.

Natural events were experienced by people all over the world. Most early civilizations developed myths to explain how the universe and everything in it formed, as well as where people went when they died.

THE AFTERLIFE

The ancient Greeks believed that the souls of the dead traveled to the Underworld. First, they had to cross the River Styx. The ferryman, Charon, charged a coin to take them across to Hades, so the Greeks placed coins in the mouths of the deceased.

Like the Greeks, the Norse believed in an afterlife. They imagined that there were two underworlds. One was for most people, including all women. The other was for mighty warriors. The Norse told stories of winged women called Valkyries who carried dead warriors to a magnificent hall with a roof made of shields called Valhalla. At Valhalla, the men would feast and drink and be waited upon by the Valkyries.

In one Greek myth, Tartarus was a region of the underworld where only the wickedest people were sent. One of these people was King Sisyphus, who killed his guests. He was forced to push a boulder up a mountainside. Just before he reached the top, Zeus made it roll back down. The king had to start again and again.

rituals: a series of actions connected with religion.

WORDS TO KNOW

The ancient Egyptians also had many myths and rituals connected to death. Egyptians believed that the dead traveled by boat to the Hall of Judgement. Here, people explained their actions on Earth.

Anubis, a god who protected the spirits of the dead, weighed each heart against a feather. If they balanced, people become immortal. If they did not, they would be eaten.

THE SEASONS

The Greeks told of Hades kidnapping Persephone to explain the change from summer to winter. The Acoma Native Americans tell a legend about a chief of the Acoma tribe with a daughter called Co-Chin. After she became the wife of the Spirit of Winter, the corn stopped growing and the Acoma began to starve. One day, Co-Chin met the Spirit of Summer. He gave her an ear of green corn and promised to bring her people more. When the Spirit of Winter saw the corn, he became angry and fought with the Spirit of Summer. But neither could win. They decided each would rule the earth for half the year.

You can read the myth at this website. How is it similar to the Greek myth?

KEYWORD PROMPTS

first people creation summer winter

HEROES AND MONSTERS

Just as Greek heroes bravely fought monsters, heroes in other cultures fought monsters as well! From Mesopotamia comes the myth of the hero Gilgamesh. He fought Humbaba, a monster with claws like a vulture and paws like a lion, who guarded a cedar forest. The Humbaba had been placed in the forest by the gods. Gilgamesh wanted to show the people that gods could be challenged. After many adventures, he learned that it was better to protect life than to kill it.

The epic poem *Beowulf* describes the heroic deeds of Beowulf, who sailed to the land of Denmark to fight a powerful monster named Grendel. Grendel had been attacking Denmark for many years. Beowulf killed Grendel using only his strength, and later battled the monster's mother.

From England comes the story of St. George and the Dragon. Saint George was a knight born in the Mediterranean. He set out to save the daughter of the King of Egypt, who was going to be sacrificed to a dragon. Saint George drove his sword into the dragon, but it could not pierce the beast's scales. He struck the dragon under its wing, where there are no scales, and won.

STEALING FIRE

In one Greek myth, the god Prometheus stole fire from Zeus to give to man. When Zeus learned of his crime, he punished Prometheus by chaining him to a large rock. Each day, an eagle feasted upon his liver, and each night, his liver grew back.

Native American tribes also tell of trickster characters stealing fire to give to people. One story from the Seminole tribe says that once the world was a cold place. Only one tribe knew the secret of fire. They would not share it with anyone.

Each year, they held a large festival. People danced around the fire, but they could never get close enough to learn its secret. One year, a crafty rabbit came to the celebration and stole some fire. Since then, all tribes have had fire.

THEN & NOW

THEN: People believed that gods controlled certain aspects of the world. These aspects reflected their personalities.

NOW: The names of gods are used by modern companies and sports teams to reflect qualities or values they aspire to.

WORDS TO KNOW

Bible: a book with sacred writings generally accepted by Christians as inspired by God.

ark: a large boat.

The Kayapo tribe in the Amazon River Basin tells a tale about a young boy called Botoque who became stranded at the top of a cliff with no food or water. A jaguar found him and invited him to his home. To Botoque's amazement, the house was heated by fire. The Jaguar taught him about fire. When Botoque began to miss his family, the Jaguar allowed him to return home if he promised not to reveal the secret of fire. Botoque did not keep his promise and stole the fire.

FLOODS

The Greek god Prometheus learned of Zeus's plan to punish the people of Earth with a flood. Prometheus advised his son, Deucalion, to build a boat. Deucalion carried out his father's instructions. When the rain came, it flooded the land for nine days and nine nights. The boat came to rest on Mount Parnassus. Deucalion created new men and women by throwing rocks into the water.

WHAT MOVIE WAS POPULAR IN ANCIENT GREECE?

Troy story!

The Bible tells of a great flood that happened when God was angry with evil on Earth. God instructed a man, Noah, to build an ark and fill it with two of every animal. Noah listened to God. The rain fell for 40 days and 40 nights. The ark finally came to rest on Mount Ararat. After the waters receded, God promised Noah that life would never be destroyed by a flood again.

From India comes the story of the first man, Manu. While Manu was washing his hands in a small bowl of water, a tiny fish spoke to him. The fish asked to be moved to a larger bowl of water.

WHY COULDN'T HADES BE A COMIC?

He bored everyone to death.

As the fish grew, Manu kept moving it until the fish grew so large that only the sea would contain it. The grateful fish revealed that he was the creator, Brahma.

Brahma warned Manu of a great flood. Brahma told him to build a large ship so that he could save himself and the seeds of every plant on Earth. Brahma, in the form of the fish, led Manu's boat to the top of the Himalayas. After the flood waters receded, Manu was given a wife.

COMPARE AND CONTRAST

How was the world created?	
Greek Mythology	In the beginning, there was Chaos. After Chaos came Gaia, the Earth; Eros, love; and Tartarus the Underworld.
Chinese Mythology	At the beginning of time, an egg contained the universe. After 18,000 years, the egg broke and the giant Pangu emerged.
Norse Mythology	In the beginning, there was a land of flames called Muspelheim, a land of fog and ice called Nieflheim and Ginnungagap, a huge emptiness in the center.
The Bible	Earth was without form until God spoke and separated light from dark.

Interest in ancient Greece has never gone away. We still study ancient Greek artists, mathematicians, philosophers, and scientists. We can explore grand Greek buildings and temples. Every two years, we enjoy the traditions of the Olympic Games.

Perhaps best of all are the hundreds of myths about Greek gods and goddesses, fierce soldiers, rich kings, and monsters. All of them remain with us today!

INVESTIGATE!

It's time to consider and discuss the Essential Question: Why do cultures tell similar stories to explain events people don't understand?

PROJECT!

MAKE A MODEL OF EARTH

The ancient Greeks believed that the gods created the seasons. In this experiment, you will make a model of the earth to see how the earth's tilt causes the seasons.

SUPPLIES

* computer with Internet access and printer
* pen
* scissors
* glue
* large Styrofoam ball
* pencil
* marker
* rubber band
* table lamp

1 Print out a map of the continents. The dimensions will vary based on the size of your globe. You can use this website.

- mapsofworld.com/world-maps/world-map-for-kids.html

2 Make a dot on the map to indicate where you live. Cut the continents out and glue them to your Styrofoam globe.

3 Push the pencil through the center of your globe. Label the South Pole at the bottom and the North Pole at the top. For the earth's equator, put a rubber band around the middle of your globe.

4 Dim the lights. Turn on your table lamp as the sun.

5 Hold your globe near the light and tilt the North Pole slightly one way. Slowly rotate your globe counterclockwise around the lamp. Stop every quarter. Look at where the light falls. What season is it?

PROJECT!

6 Decide what season it is where you live. Think about what season it is in both the Northern Hemisphere and the Southern Hemisphere. Write down your observations.

Northern Hemisphere: the half of the earth north of the equator.

Southern Hemisphere: the half of the earth south of the equator.

axis: the imaginary line through the North and South Poles that the earth rotates around.

WORDS TO KNOW

THINK ABOUT IT: The earth rotates with a tilt on its axis. As it rotates, it also orbits the sun. Sometimes, the Northern Hemisphere is tilted toward the sun, and sometimes the Southern Hemisphere is tilted toward the sun. The tilt influences the seasons because it determines how much sun falls on that part of the earth.

PROJECT!

GREAT FLOOD EXPERIMENT

Cultures all over the world tell of a great flood. You can experiment with paper cup model homes, a slope, a river, and rain from a water bottle to explore the science behind floods.

SUPPLIES

* large waterproof container
* soil
* 4 small paper cups
* waterproof markers
* pebbles
* sticks
* small water bottle

1 In your container, build a slope with the soil. It needs to be steeper at the back of the container than the front. Leave one bottom corner of the container empty. This will be where you pour in your water.

2 Turn the cups upside down, Draw house features on each cup.

3 Place your cup houses at different levels in the container and at different distances to the river. Add pebbles and sticks to the soil.

4 Slowly pour water into the empty space for your river. Fill the river until the water is level with the land. Poke holes in the bottom of the water bottle. Let it rain by shaking the bottle all over.

THINGS TO NOTICE: What happens to the river when you make it rain? What happens to the homes on lower ground as the water level rises? What do you notice about homes built on higher ground?

CREATE A STORY: A BIRTHDAY PRESENT FOR ZEUS

Use words from the glossary and text to create a silly story.

- noun: a person, place, or thing.
- plural noun: more than one person, place, or thing.
- adjective: a word that describes a noun.
- verb: an action word.

Heracles was the son of Zeus. He was ______ (ADJECTIVE) than anyone. One day, Heracles set out on a/an ______ (ADJECTIVE) ______ (NOUN). He wanted to get Zeus a gift for his birthday. He wanted it to be the ______ (ADJECTIVE) gift that Zeus had ever seen. Heracles traveled to the underworld to find a one-of-a-kind present. He was sure to find a ______ (ADJECTIVE) gift there! But a beautiful golden eagle blocked his way. Heracles shooed it away. He went through dark ______ (PLURAL NOUN). In the darkness, a ______ (NOUN) attacked him. Finally, Heracles reached the River Styx. More than forty ______ (PLURAL NOUN) chased after him. The golden eagle dropped ______ (NOUN) on his head. But Heracles ______ (VERB) onto the ferryman Charon's boat. On the other side, Heracles met with Hades and asked him for ______ (PROPER NOUN) and Cerberus. Hades looked at his chewed shoes and throne and agreed.

Cerberus came with Heracles to Mount Olympus, but he missed ______ (NOUN) and ______ (NOUN). And Zeus, god of ______ (NOUN), did not like it when Cerberus chewed his ______ (PLURAL NOUN). When the guests sang "Happy Birthday," Cerberus ______ (VERB) loudly. When Zeus began to open his presents, Cerberus ______ (VERB). Then, Cerberus chewed the ______ (NOUN) on Zeus's chariot! Hercules had to bring Cerberus back to ______ (NOUN). But on his way home, the same golden eagle blocked his path. Heracles had an idea. Zeus was ______ (ADJECTIVE) with the golden eagle. Heracles was happy that he had found a gift for Zeus.

A

Acropolis: a rocky ledge high above Athens, home to ancient buildings, including the Parthenon.

altar: a raised table used for religious purposes.

archaeologist: a scientist who studies ancient people through the objects they left behind.

ark: a large boat.

astronomy: the study of the sun, moon, stars, planets, and space.

axis: the imaginary line through the North and South Poles that the earth rotates around.

B

BCE: put after a date, BCE stands for Before Common Era and counts down to zero. CE stands for Common Era and counts up from zero. These nonreligious terms correspond to BC and AD. This book was printed in 2016 CE.

Bible: a book with sacred writings generally accepted by Christians as inspired by God.

boustrophedon: a system of writing on alternate lines and in opposite directions.

C

chaos: a state of complete confusion.

circa: around that year. Abbreviated with a c (c.610–546 BCE).

citizen: a person who has all the rights and responsibilities that come with being a full member of a country. In Athens, only adult males could be citizens.

civilization: a community of people that is advanced in art, science, and government.

compass rose: a circle drawn on a map to show north, south, east, and west.

compound pulley: a system of fixed and movable pulleys that work together.

constellation: a group of stars in the sky that resembles a certain shape, such as the Big Dipper. There are 88 official constellations in the sky.

Corinthian: a style of architecture featuring decorative columns with leaves, flowers, and scrolls.

culture: the beliefs and way of life of a group of people.

current: the steady flow of water or air in one direction.

curse: words that people believe cause harm.

D

Dark Age: a time when a civilization undergoes a decline. The Dark Age in Greece lasted from 1100 to 700 BCE.

demi-god: a person with one parent who is human and one parent who is a god.

democracy: a system of government where the people choose who will represent and govern them.

discus: a circular disc that was thrown by athletes in ancient Greece and by the god Apollo.

Doric: a style of architecture featuring simple columns topped by squares.

E

epic: a long story that celebrates the adventures and achievements of a god or hero in verse.

exiled: forced to leave one's country.

F

forge: a furnace where metal is heated up to make tools or other objects.

fresco: a painting made on fresh, wet plaster.

frieze: a carved band of stone or marble that often tells a story or shows characters from a myth.

furrow: a long, narrow trail in the soil.

G

geography: the study of the earth and its features, especially the shape of the land and the effect of human activity on the earth.

gorge: a narrow valley between hills or mountains, usually with steep rocky walls and a stream running through it.

H

harmony: the arrangement of parts in pleasing relation to each other.

I

immortal: describes a person who cannot die.

Ionic: a style of architecture featuring slender columns with scroll-like details at the top.

J

jury: a group of people, called jurors, who hear a case in court. Jurors give their opinion, called a verdict.

L

lever: a bar that is used to lift a heavy load.

literature: written work such as poems, plays, and novels.

M

manga: a style of comic book from Japan.

mortar: a building material that hardens when it dries. It is used like glue to hold bricks and stones together.

Mount Olympus: the home of the Greek gods.

Mycenaean Age: a Greek civilization that flourished from 1650 to 1200 BCE.

myth: a traditional story that expresses the beliefs and values of a group of people.

N

narcissism: the feeling of being overly interested in your own appearance.

Norse: people from Denmark, Norway, and Sweden.

Northern Hemisphere: the half of the earth north of the equator.

O

ode: a poem set to music that celebrates a person, place, or thing.

offering: an object given to the gods as a gift.

Olympic Games: a global sporting event held every two years. In ancient Greece, these events took place every four years in Olympia, Greece, in honor of Zeus.

oracle: a spiritual advisor believed to be able to predict the future.

orchestra: a stage where Greek singers, actors, and musicians acted out the drama in a play.

ostracism: being excluded from a group.

P

pantheon: a group of gods belonging to a religion.

patron: a person or supernatural being that is believed to support and protect a person, group, or place.

pediment: the triangular piece on the front of some buildings at the top.

Peloponnesus: the southern region of ancient Greece, where the Mycenaean civilization developed.

Persian Empire: a large empire to the south and east of Greece.

phenomenon: something seen or observed.

philosopher: someone who thinks about and questions the way things are in the world.

pivot: the center on which something turns or balances.

plains: large, flat areas of land.

polis: a Greek city–state.

prophecy: a prediction of the future.

pulley: a wheel with a groove for a rope used to lift a load.

Q

quarry: a pit where stone is cut for building.

R

riddle: a puzzle that is asked as a question.

rituals: a series of actions connected with religion.

S

sacrifice: an offering of an animal to the gods.

satyr: a mythical creature that is half man and half goat.

shrine: a special, religious place.

society: an organized community of people with shared laws, traditions, and values.

Southern Hemisphere: the half of the earth south of the equator.

stoa: a long covered walkway.

supernatural: something that cannot be explained using the laws of science.

T

tectonic plates: large slabs of the earth's crust that are in constant motion. The plates move on the hot, melted layer of earth below.

tide: the daily rise and fall of ocean water.

Titans: the first family on Earth.

toga: a loose, one-piece garment worn by men in ancient Greece and ancient Rome.

trident: a spear with three sharp points.

V

votive: a small offering to the gods, such as a coin.

Z

zodiac: the 12 sections in the sky that ancient astronomers used to describe the path of the sun.

BOOKS

Bolt Simmons, Lisa M. *Daily Life in Ancient Greece*. Capstone, 2014.

Bordessa, Kris. *Tools of the Ancient Greeks: A Kid's Guide to the History & Science of Life in Ancient Greece*. Nomad Press, 2006.

Caper, William. *Ancient Greece: An Interactive History Adventure*. Capstone, 2010.

Chislom, Jane, Lisa Miles, and Struan Reid. *Encyclopedia of Ancient Greece*. Usborne Books, 2007.

Connolly, Peter. *The Ancient Greece of Odysseus*. Oxford University Press, 2002.

Connolly, Peter. *Greece and Rome at War*. Frontline Books, 2012.

D'Aulaire, Ingri, and d'Aulaire, Edgar Parin. *D'Aulaires' Book of Greek Myths*. Delacorte Books for Young Readers, 1992.

Green Jen. *Hail! Ancient Greeks*. Crabtree Publishing, 2010.

Jennings, Ken. *Greek Mythology*. Little Simon, 2014.

Lupton, Hugh. *Demeter and Persephone*. Barefoot Books, 2013.

MacDonald, Fiona. *I Wonder Why Greeks Built Temples: And Other Questions About Ancient Greece*. Kingfisher, 2012.

Nardo, Dan. *The Epics of Greek Mythology*. Compass Point Books, 2011.

Newman, Sandra. *Ancient Greece (True Books: Ancient Civilizations)*. Scholastic, 2010.

Ollhoff, Jim. *Greek Mythology*. ABDO & Daughters, 2011.

Pearson, Anne. *DK Eyewitness Books: Ancient Greece*. DK Children, 2014.

WEBSITES

A to Z Kids Stuff Ancient Greece: atozkidsstuff.com/greece.html

Ancient Greece: ancientgreece.com/s/Main_Page

Ancient Greece - The British Museum: ancientgreece.co.uk

BBC Bitesize - Ancient Greece: bbc.co.uk/education/topics/z87tn39

BBC Learning School Radio: bbc.co.uk/learning/schoolradio/subjects/history/ancient_greek_myths

Cyber Sleuth Kids Ancient Civilizations: cybersleuth-kids.com/sleuth/History/Ancient_Civilizations/Greece/index.htm

DK Find Out - Ancient Greece: dkfindout.com/uk/history/ancient-greece

Gods and Goddesses of Ancient Greece: greek-gods.info

History for Kids Guide to Ancient Greece: historyforkids.net/ancient-greece.html

Hellenic Ministry of Culture and Sport: www.culture.gr/culture/eindex.jsp

Mr. Donn Greek Mythology for Kids: greece.mrdonn.org/myths.html

National Geographic Kids: ngkids.co.uk/history/10-facts-about-the-ancient-greeks

The Children's University of Manchester: childrensuniversity.manchester.ac.uk/interactives/history/greece

Thessaloniki Science Center & Technology Museum: noesis.edu.gr/en

Time for Kids: timeforkids.com/destination/greece/sightseeing

MUSEUMS

Getty Villa: getty.edu/visit

Los Angeles County Museum: lacma.org/art/collection/greek-roman-and-etruscan-art

Museum of Fine Arts, Boston: mfa.org/collections/ancient-world

The Cleveland Museum of Art: clevelandart.org/art/departments/greek-and-roman-art

The Metropolitan Museum of Art: metmuseum.org/about-the-museum/museum-departments/curatorial-departments/greek-and-roman-art

The Parthenon in Nashville: nashville.gov/Parks-and-Recreation/Parthenon.aspx

University of Pennsylvania Museum of Archaeology and Anthropology: penn.museum

QR Code Glossary

page 2: Merriam-Webster.com

page 22: ancient-origins.net/ancient-technology/ingenious-invention-tower-winds-001902

page 25: 151.12.58.141/virtualexhibition/spider.html

page 27: ancient.eu/article/390

page 32: artsy.net/artwork/unknown-rome-italy-lazio-europe-mosaic-floor-with-head-of-medusa

page 40: english.illinois.edu/-people-/faculty/debaron/482/482readings/phaedrus.html

page 56: metmuseum.org/art/online-features/metkids/videos/MetKids-How-can-I-recognize-ancient-Greek-architecture

page 58: britishmuseum.org/explore/galleries/ancient_greece_and_rome/room_18_greece_parthenon_scu.aspx?fromShortUrl

page 67: windows2universe.org/mythology/scorpius.html

page 74: firstpeople.us/FP-Html-Legends/Creation_Of_Summer_And_Winter-Acoma.html

ESSENTIAL QUESTIONS:

Introduction: What are some characteristics of Greek myths?

Chapter One: Why did the Greeks use myths to explain natural disasters?

Chapter Two: Do stories told today contain lessons? Can you think of examples?

Chapter Three: Do Greek heroes share certain characteristics? Why?

Chapter Four: How did the ancient Greeks build such impressive structures without modern machinery?

Chapter Five: How is the civilization of ancient Greece important today?

Chapter Six: Why do cultures tell similar stories to explain events people don't understand?

INDEX